FIGHTING THE GOOD FIGHT

Scriptural Responses to Controversial Topics

Sylvia Alexander-Jones

Lighthouse Publications, Inc.

Fighting the Good Fight:
Scriptural Responses to Controversial Topics
by Sylvia Alexander-Jones
Printed in the United States of America
ISBN 1-933656-07-7

Unless otherwise indicated, Bible quotations are taken from the King James Version.

Publisher
Lighthouse Publications, Inc.
2028 Larkin Avenue
Elgin, IL 60123
(847) 697-6788
www.Lighthouse-Publications.com

Cover Design and Layout
Scott Wallis & Associates
2028 Larkin Avenue
Elgin, IL 60123
(847) 468-1457
www.ScottWallis.net

Dedication

*T*o the Holy Spirit for being my Counselor, my Friend. To my son, Benjamin, for being so patient, and to my husband, Barry, for those needed things.

God has more than one way to see a job through. He knows exactly what he wants to do, even if it means stretching my potential to do it. I trust Him.

Foreword

*F*ighting the Good Fight is an inspiring devotional that addresses varied life topics, ranging from marriage and singleness to stress and self-esteem. This unique compilation of Scripture and practical insight offers encouragement and guidance to contemporary Christians.

Spiritual and emotional issues that affect our lives are addressed in God's teachings, but often we don't know where to find the words we so desperately need. Here readers will find extensive guidance from the Bible, as well as sensible summary advice. As we face the challenging questions that arise in our families and communities and experience our need to learn more about God, *Fighting the Good Fight* is a valuable and beneficial resource.

Contents

SECTION I

SECTION 1

Chapter One
Abortion
Conception
Children
Parenting

Chapter Two
Adultery
Homosexuality
Infidelity
Satan

Chapter Three
Dating
Divorce
Marriage
Singleness

Chapter Four
Angels
God
Holy Spirit
Jesus

Chapter Five
Family
Generational Curses
Unity

Chapter Six
Poem
Authority
Power

Chapter Seven
Death
Grief
Resurrection

Chapter Eight
Healing
Hope
Longevity

Chapter One

Abortion

*W*hen my father and mother forsake me, then the Lord will take me up (Ps. 27:10).

Forsake me not, O Lord: O my God, be not far from me. Make haste to help me, O Lord, my salvation. (Ps. 38:21-22).

I will praise Thee; for I am fearfully and wonderfully made: marvelous are Thy works; and that my soul knoweth right well. My substance was not hid from Thee, when I was made in secret, and curiously wrought in the lowest parts of the earth. Thine eyes did see my substance, yet being imperfect; and in Thy book all my members were written, which in continuance were fashioned, when as yet there was none of them (Ps. 139:13-16).

Trust in the Lord with all thine heart; and lean not unto thine own understanding. In all thy ways, acknowledge Him, and He shall direct thy paths (Prov. 3:5-6).

Before I formed thee in the belly, I knew thee; and before thou camest forth out of the womb, I sanctified thee, and I ordained thee a prophet unto the nations (Jer. 1:5).

If we confess our sins, He is faithful and just to forgive us our sins, and to cleanse us from all unrighteousness (1 Jn. 1:9).

...And Yet, a Baby's Born

Thine eyes did see my substance, yet being imperfect; and in Thy book all my members were written, which in continuance were fashioned, when as yet there was none of them (Ps. 139:16).

The day I laid eyes on my newborn son, I was thrilled, and could not wait to take him home to nurture him and watch him grow. Just knowing that God's love for us enables us to produce another being like ourselves is reason enough for me to want to bring a child into this world. Besides, it is truly amazing to watch bits and pieces of yourself expressed through your little one as time progresses.

Whenever I asked the Lord to enable me to write a little about abortion, a situation involving a young woman and an unwanted pregnancy was placed at my feet. Knowing very little about the fear that works its way in the mind of a person who becomes pregnant unwillingly caught me by surprise, and for some time, I wondered how I could be of any help to her. Nevertheless, I did my best to encourage her whenever she confided in me, and when she did not, I asked the Lord to strengthen her weakness.

There were times she looked discouraged, and no doubt felt very much alone. Why, even though she was old enough to take responsibility for her own actions, she feared telling her own mother about her big "mistake." You know, I used to be critical of people, women particularly, who thought that contentment and wholeness could be found in one night between two sheets with someone she really didn't care for, and who cared even less for her. Later I learned that if it were not for the awesome grace of God perhaps, I too would search for peace and wholeness in an empty place.

I recall staring into her eyes whenever she confided in me, hoping that she might see a little light at the end of what appeared to be a dark tunnel. But perhaps the fear of having another child, unwed with a poor income was reason enough for her to seek abortion as a means of escape. She wasted no time in letting me know this. It did appear to me that she felt no shame, no conviction whatsoever; she simply stared back at me as though I were the one struggling with this decision and needing to do the right thing. She may have been hoping that I might view the situation as she did, as if my thoughts on the matter were of that much importance.

I thought over the matter for a while and realized that anything I said might have a strong bearing on the matter. But suddenly, I felt something leaping from my heart and this gave me the courage to speak; perhaps I was speaking for the many women out there who would love to hear the words,

"Congratulations, you're pregnant;" women who shed tears over the thought of not being able to conceive.

Or maybe... just maybe, I thought about myself, who at that particular time was unable to conceive a child at will. At just the thought of it, I braced up as though what I was about to say to her was given to me by angel Gabriel himself.

"What if God has appointed your little son or daughter to be one of this world's great teachers, a Scientist, one gifted to help change the lives of children in all walks of life? Or perhaps, He's calling your little one from the womb to become a great doctor of medicine, one touched by the hand of God to cure illnesses from ages past."

I continued, "How about an athlete, one who's blessed with the swiftness of an angel, superior in strength and character? Listen, who's to say that this child in your womb will not bless your later years with joy, prosperity and gratefulness to God for a mother's work well done? Tell me, are you going to stand in the way of this individual's work on this earth?"

She did not say a word at this time, but stared at me in bewilderment, as though what I had said sounded out of this world; that which made me eligible for the "not quite human club." But, after a while, I learned that she had decided to have her baby.

God's peace be with you!

Point of Contact

Check out Christian help groups, organizations, and so on. Associate with persons who made it through unplanned pregnancies. Be associated with someone who encourages you and will enable you to focus on things that are lovely and lovable.

Conception

And God blessed them, and God said unto them, be fruitful and multiply, and replenish the earth, and subdue it (Gen. 1:28).

He maketh the barren woman to keep house, and to be a joyful mother of children (Ps. 113:9).

Thou hast well seen: for I will hasten My word to perform it (Jer. 1:12).

Call unto Me and I will answer thee, and show Thee great and mighty things, which thou knowest not (Jer. 33:3).

And whatsoever ye shall ask in My Name, that will I do, that the Father may be glorified in the Son (Jn. 14:13).

Casting all your care upon Him; for He careth for you (1 Pt. 5:7).

Hannah's Hope

Conception is truly a wonderful gift from God. To those who are able to plan their families according to the plan of God without any interruptions, I say, "you are truly blessed." But twice blessed are those who are trusting God for the fulfillment of a promise that the joy they're expecting may be complete.

Remember those wonderful women in the Bible who received a blessing because of their tenacious faith? Wait a minute! For those women, conception was no simple accomplishment – surely, there were interruptions.

In Genesis 18:10, God promised a child to Abraham and his wife Sarah, even though she was much too old to conceive. Why, even the sound of this life long dream caused her to break forth in laughter. Perhaps she was convinced that the delay meant God's denial and after all this time it was impossible; therefore the thought of it all seemed downright hilarious to Sarah. Surely, God could have blessed Sarah's womb when she was much younger and caused her to become pregnant, but God had a plan for her son Isaac's life for the time that he was born.

Now, what about Hannah? In my opinion, Hannah's desire to have a child represents all women who are longing for conception. Hannah walks into God's house, a sanctuary, like an old inebriated woman. Picture her, if you will, with me for a moment. A young woman, longing for the love of a baby, walks in the sanctuary without makeup, scratching the right side of her hip, then looking down at her dusty feet as she brushes her sandal against her garment. The clothes she was wearing looked as if she had spent not only the night, but the entire week in them. Her countenance was so disfigured, that the Priest could only imagine that she had been drinking. After sitting down, she realized that she could not bear the pain anymore, so she began to pour her heart out to God. I would imagine her prayer went something like this:

"'O Lord, you are not a man that you should lie' (Num. 23:19), 'you said that children are a gift from you, the fruit of the womb is your reward' (Ps. 127:3). 'I need you Father; surely, I can make it in this life without any children because you are more than enough; but since your promises to me are yea and Amen' (2 Cor. 1:20), 'I ask that you do not over look me this day, do not forsake the works of your hand' (Ps. 138:8); 'whatever it takes Father, whatever it takes, I'll do it. I humble myself before you, my King, and my God– Amen.'"

Immediately after Hannah's prayer, again I would imagine she started laughing, for her faith enabled her to see what she did not have yet in the natural. Later, Hannah conceived and Samuel was born to her and her husband Elkanah, and she had professed to the Lord, "whatever it takes!" Hannah dedicated her son to the Lord's service.

Just before the birth of Jesus, God performed another awesome miracle and blessed Elizabeth, who was cursed with barrenness. God told her husband Zechariah that he would grant them a son and He did. The husband as priest of his home, bowing his head in prayer is a wonderful thing to see. I would imagine that his petition was like sweet smelling incense before God, and through it the anointing that destroys yokes.

Look, for the child of God there is no curse; Jesus bore that curse in His own body when He hung on the cross (Gal. 3:13). I would imagine there were others who received the miracle of conception; some are recorded, others are not. Nevertheless, God is still in the business of performing the impossible. Ask Him, trust Him, and wait on Him so that your joy may be full.

Point of Contact

Whatever it takes, consider discussing with one another the overall cost of infertility check-ups, and then write out a budget in order that you might see a clear path. However, time alone with God will give you a peace of mind and clear direction.

Children

For He shall give His angels charge over thee, to keep thee in all thy ways (Ps. 91:11).

Trust in the Lord with all thine heart, and lean not unto thine own understanding. In all thy ways acknowledge Him, and He shall direct thy paths (Prov. 3:5-6).

But thus saith the Lord, "Even the captives of the terrible shall be away, and the prey of the terrible shall be delivered: for I will contend with him that contendeth with thee, and I will save thy children" (Is. 49:25).

And all thy children shall be taught of the Lord; and great shall be the peace of thy children (Is. 54:13).

Children, obey your parents in the Lord: for this is right (Eph. 6:1).

Honour thy father and mother; which is the first commandment with promise; that it may be well with thee, and thou mayest live long on the earth (Eph. 6:2-3).

Casting all your care upon Him; for He careth for you (1 Pt. 5:7).

Christct Cadets

Ye are of God, little children, and have overcome them: because greater is He that is in you, than he that is in the world (1 Jn. 4:4).

Our children are our most prized possession, and it seems that no matter what we have or have not accomplished as far as our successes are concerned, we can look on our children and think: "I've accomplished something in this life." This the enemy knows so very well, therefore he is out to destroy man's seed.

There's something of which we should be aware, and it is this: the battles that we hear about concerning our young people are not natural ones. It isn't about gangs, violence, hormones, and guns in school... not really. Those things are simply smoke screens the enemy draws on to focus our attention from him, the real killer; while he continues to shatter the lives of these, God's chosen vessels.

Surely we know that his overall plan is to steal, kill and destroy (Jn. 10:10); but we must also keep in mind that it is the little foxes that spoil the vines (Songs 2:15). Those things in which we as parents, guardians and leaders allow our children to dabble; things that are entertaining to young minds but destined to send innocent victims towards a fatal end.

One day, while cleaning my son's room, the Lord instructed me to rid his toy box of all those playthings with demonic-like features; even those that look like monsters, as well as comic books that revealed destructive goings-on. At first I thought to test the spirit, to make sure that it was the Lord and not my old carnal nature simply wanting its own way which was tired of looking at the hideous faces and bodies of those creatures portrayed as toys.

But, the fact of the matter is, the enemy will use any means necessary to enter a home. Therefore, anything that attracts his demons was reason enough for me to obey the Spirit of God and get rid of those disgusting toys. You see, the devil isn't playing any games. He is out to destroy the seed of man even if he has to use every deceptive tool in his grab bag. For those who think he is simply an impersonator of an exceptional intelligent being gone bad: beware.

This evil trickster is cunning, wicked, and worse yet, persistent. Look, this may come as a shock to most, but he'll even go as far as to use your own precious little "angels" to rebel against you in your attempt to kick him out of your home. However, keep in mind that our "big brother" Jesus took care of him over two thousand years ago and put a bad hurt on him. Therefore, in these final hours let us remember to do our part, and know that from the days of John the Baptist until now, the kingdom of heaven suffereth violence, and the violent take it by force (Mat.11:12).

Point of Contact

Raise up a standard against the enemy, no matter what form he takes. Time alone with God will enable you as a couple or even as a single parent to discover wholesome ways to redirect whatever mental stronghold might be influencing your child. Don't give up!

Parenting

And these words, which I command thee this day, shall be in thine heart: And thou shalt teach them when thou sittest in thine house, and when thou walkest by the way, and when thou liest down, and when thou risest up (Deut. 6:6-7).

Chasten thy son while there is hope, and let not thy soul spare for his crying (Prov. 19:18).

And all thy children shall be taught of the Lord; and great shall be the peace of thy children (Is. 54:13).

But Jesus said, "Suffer little children, and forbid them not, to come unto Me: for of such is the kingdom of heaven" (Mt. 19:14).

Fathers provoke not your children to anger, lest they be discouraged (Col. 3:21).

Parent Letter

Train up a child in the way he should go: and when he is old, he will not depart from it (Prov. 22:6).

Whenever a teacher sends a letter home to parents concerning a child he or she initially informs them of that child's strengths, as well as weaknesses. He or she being the overseer may point out their concerns as to that child's outlook in the area of participation, activities, and behavior, and if the child is exceptionally gifted, his or her nutritional habits as well. If by chance the child lacks any of the particulars, the parents are encouraged to focus on a strategic course of action.

The Whole Child

Years ago, whenever I first sat down to mingle with the computer, I was puzzled. It didn't take long for me to understand that I was computer illiterate. Look! Back then, you could hand me paper and pen and it was as good as done. But, since the world we live in is constantly changing, we must be able to change with it, without sacrificing those necessary things.

One day, while going to pick up my son from school, the Lord ministered to me concerning spiritual illiteracy in children. He made use of my lack of computer knowledge as a clear illustration of what He wanted me to understand. Naturally speaking, any caring parent will do whatever is necessary for the well being of their children; to this we learn that prayer, even declaring the word of God over their lives is essentially important.

Encouraging our children to acknowledge their dependence on God may very well aid them further towards a successful future, and strengthen them against the camouflage attacks of the deceiver.

Point of Contact

Be a parent to your child at all times; but be a friend to your child when they need a friend. Be a listener, an encourager, an advisor, a wound healer, and a disciplinarian so that they might bless you all the days of their lives.

Chapter Two

Adultery

*T*hou shalt not commit adultery (Ex. 20:14).

But whoso committeth adultery with a woman lacketh understanding: he that doeth it destroyed his own soul (Prov. 6:32).

But I say unto you that whosoever looketh on a woman to lust after her hath committed adultery with her already in his heart (Mt. 5:28).

And Jesus said unto her, neither do I condemn thee: go, and sin no more (Jn. 8:11).

If ye continue in My word, then are ye My disciples indeed; and ye shall know the truth, and the truth shall make you free (Jn. 8:31-32).

Can't Touch This

...And I have come down to deliver them out of the hand of the Egyptians (Ex. 3:8).

What's up, "lady Jez;" calling again, and so soon? Tell me, what is it about an adulteress that makes her seek after the affections of a married man. You know your queen mother Jezebel would be so proud of you the way you lurk around at the threshold of sin. O, did you remember to bring your ammo, 'cause girl, you are gonna need it. You see, I am armed and dangerous, and there are more fighting *for* me than against me.

For a very short period, a woman phoned my home as often as she wanted, to the point where it appeared to me that she had nothing better to do. In my opinion, she possessed very little dignity – for what other reason would one choose to be a bondwoman. You know, it has been said through the years that whenever a person was on the make for another's spouse, the victim spouse was always the last to know. But, let me tell you something, if you put the Lord first in all of your affairs, he'll make you to be the head and not the tail, above only and not beneath (Deut. 28:13).

At first, her calls were frustrating, because for me, the thought of having to defend my title as "first lady" was something I found to be totally unnecessary. Soon, I began to express signs of this frustration verbally. That's right, I felt the need to go there, and why not?

After all, whenever the devil whispers a suggestion of wrongdoing to anyone who happens to be unguarded, that person does not step up to the plate without all of the necessary equipment (carnal readiness). But then, instead of following after my carnal thinking, I chose to do what any real warrior would: I got down on my knees and humbled myself before the Mighty God, and after a little while, I returned fully armed to destroy even the memory of the daughter of Jezebel.

Point of Contact

If your eyes cause you to sin, close them and look the other way. If your hands cause you to sin, push away the temptation like a swimmer propels water to swim upstream. If your imagination causes you to sin, renew it with the Word of God.

Homosexuality

Because of this, God gave them over to shameful lusts. Even their women exchanged natural relations for unnatural ones. In the same way the men also abandoned natural relations with women and were inflamed with lust for one another. Men committed indecent acts with other men, and received in themselves the due penalty for their perversion (Rom. 1:26-27).

In Whom we have redemption through His blood, the forgiveness of sins, according to the riches of His grace (Eph. 1:7).

That the God of our Lord Jesus Christ, the Father of glory, may give unto you the spirit of wisdom and revelation in the knowledge of Him. The eyes of your understanding being enlightened; that ye may know what is the hope of His calling, and what the riches of the glory of His inheritance in the saints (Eph. 1:17-18).

That He would grant you, according to the riches of His glory, to be strengthened with might by His Spirit in the inner man (Eph. 3:16).

And to know the love of Christ, which passeth knowledge, that ye might be filled with all the fullness of God (Eph. 3:19).

Wanna Walk Like You

So God created man in His own image, in the image of God created He him; male and female created He them (Gen. 1:27).

Now here is some good news! God created each one of us in His image. Therefore, none of us should ever have to struggle with an identity crisis. But, that is not so! Wanna know why? Because, the enemy comes against God's handiwork.

One day while I was stepping out of my car, I glanced into the back seat to see if there was anything I needed to take into the house; just as I turned, a catalog lying on the seat caught my attention. On the cover of this catalog was a picture of a very attractive woman with very distinguished features. Features that reflect the inner beauty of a virtuous woman, but then again the distinctive glow of a God-fearing man. Respectfully speaking, her features, though beautiful were like that of a man; for some strange reason, Christ came to mind. While sitting there just staring at the picture on this catalog, I could not help but think of the beauty and creativity of God. We, both male and female, are a vivid representation of the unseen Christ.

An old friend of mine has a son who lives a homosexual lifestyle. This young man never really seemed to know whether he was coming or going as a child, thus he stepped out into this great big world having very little knowledge concerning the snares of the fowler and the traps of men. A very shy, soft-spoken child was he with a girlish grin – that which was past down to him from Mother dearest. Why, even after the years rolled by and this young boy grew into manhood, nothing seemed to change; still shy, soft-spoken, and, yes, that same girlish grin. Well, with this world the way it is, with the devil always on the prowl, and the weakness of the flesh, it wasn't difficult for passersby to mistake this once innocent little boy for a she. But, wait a minute. I thought that he was made in the image and likeness of Almighty God. So, who stole his identity, that which is hidden in Christ?

The missing identity of this young man concerned me, until I decided to bring him before the Lord in prayer, the Lord said to me, "The eyes of the world are full of darkness!" So the world stole this young man's identity, because it looked on his outer appearance and labeled him. The devil stole this young man's identity because he's out to kill, steal and destroy (Jn. 10:10). Before you know it, his flesh yielded to its own weakness and gave up the fight. But my prayer for you is that you be transformed by the renewing of your mind (Rom. 12:2).

Point of Contact

Be honest with God about whether you enjoy your lifestyle or not. A relationship with Christ in the Spirit of truth will open the door to a whole new you, someone that you never thought existed.

Infidelity

Let thy fountain be blessed: and rejoice with the wife of thy youth.
Let her be as the loving hind and pleasant roe; let her breasts

satisfy thee at all times; and be thou ravished always with her love. For the ways of man are before the eyes of the Lord, and He pondereth all his goings (Prov. 5:18-19, 21).

Submitting yourselves one to another in the fear of God (Eph. 5:21).

Nevertheless let every one of you in particular so love his wife even as himself, and the wife see that she reverence her husband (Eph. 5:33).

To Thine Own Self Be True

Drink water from your own cistern, running water from your own well (Prov. 5:15).

When I was in junior high, and the teacher would step out of the classroom, the entire class, girls and boys alike, would also step out. Then, whenever she'd walk back in, the class would immediately find their places and the classroom was again in order. Realizing what was going on, the teacher would then say, "Children do not behave yourselves only when I am looking, but to your own self be true." In other words, do what you know is right even when no one is watching.

That's exactly what I think about whenever the word infidelity comes to mind: "Be true to yourself." The thought of a spouse betraying another is like a slap in the face on a cold day. And, to those who have at some time in life been a victim of infidelity I say, "Be encouraged!" Call me an extremist if you will, but it amazes me to know that our Lord suffered the same hurts that we do, in one form or another and was victorious. If you don't believe me, read some of the books in the New Testament. You know, whenever I am going through any kind of emotional pain, I ask the Holy Spirit to be Lord of my emotions, and if I willingly submit myself to His wisdom, He provides a cushion for the comfort of my heavy heart.

Surely, there are many hurting, betrayed persons in this world – men and women alike, who have been hurt by someone. But to you I say, "Go where the peace is, that's where the Prince of peace will be."

Point of Contact

Commit yourself to spending time with your own spouse. Laughing together, talking together, listening to one another's hopes and dreams, that the seed of friendship might begin to take root and cause love to blossom continually.

Satan

And he shewed me Joshua the high priest standing before the angel of the Lord, and Satan standing at his right hand to resist (accuse) him. (Zec. 3:1).

Satan hath desired to have you, that he may sift you as wheat (Lk. 22:31).

...The devil...was a murderer from the beginning, and abode not in the truth, because there is no truth in him. When he speaketh a lie, he speaketh of his own: for he is a liar, and the father of it (Jn. 8:44).

In fact, no one can enter a strong man's house and carry off his possessions unless he first ties up the strong man. Then he can rob his house (Mk. 3:27).

Satan himself is transformed into (masquerades as) an angel of light (2 Cor. 11:14).

...The prince of the power of the air, the spirit that now (temporarily) worketh in the children of disobedience (Eph. 2:1-2).

For we wrestle not against flesh and blood, but against principalities, against powers, against the rulers of the darkness of this world, against spiritual wickedness in high places (Eph. 6:12).

And the devil that deceived them was cast into the lake of fire and brimstone, where the beast and the false prophet are, and shall be tormented day and night forever and ever (Rev. 20:10).

Strong Man

How art thou fallen from heaven, O Lucifer, son of the morning! How art thou cut down to the ground, which didst weaken the nations! For thou hast said in thine heart, I will ascend into heaven, I will exalt my throne above the stars of God: I will sit also upon the mount of the congregation, in the sides of the north: I will ascend above the heights of the clouds; I will be like the Most High. Yet thou shalt be brought down to hell, to the sides of the pit (Is. 14:12-15).

Have you ever been engaged in spiritual warfare? Do you even know what it is like to experience an encounter with the prince of the power of the air? I do! And, although the actual encounter happened some years earlier, whenever I wrote a short story for a class project hoping to expose the wicked prince, his claws became sharper whenever he learned of my passion for pen and paper. At first, his attacks were mild, minor bouts of oppression here and there, but then as I proceeded, he became downright nasty in his attempts to sever me away from my task.

One afternoon, my husband decided that he and our son would leave in the morning for a short weekend trip to visit the folks. "Sounds good to me," I thought. After all, this trip would allow me a little time to finish some things that were overdue.

But as evening approached, I felt a little uneasy. After a while, I felt as though there was a strange presence following me around. This presence was unlike the sweet presence of the Holy Spirit– this presence was dark, unruly, and frightening, and so I was frightened. However, instead of resisting him that he might flee from me, I was the one who wanted to flee.

Let me just say that, as a young girl, my biggest fear was animals. I simply did not like animals nibbling at my feet or scratching my legs. Therefore, I am not an animal lover, especially if the animal belongs to someone else. But, during this time, I would have gladly welcomed "Bambi" to nibble on the hem of my skirt without making a fuss; anything but 'ole Beelzebub, the enemy of my soul.

Indeed, I had experienced little encounters from this wicked prince but never anything like this– I was terrified. Therefore, I did the only thing I knew to do, I fell on my knees and cried out to God in prayer, asking for His divine help and protection. Indeed, whenever we give our lives to the Lord Jesus, making Him Lord and Savior, we can boldly go to the throne, and expect to receive from Him. However, since we are merely human, and cannot see the many attacks that are assigned to come our way from time to time, we sometimes lose site of the authority that is ours through Christ Jesus. Being disturbed to the point of tears, I cried out to God in deep distress. After a while, everything around me became so quiet, you could hear a pin drop; it was as if the whole world stood still.

Then He spoke very gently saying, "Open your Bible to the Book of Ezekiel, chapter Twenty-eight." After reading this particular chapter, I rose to my feet like a warrior who was ready for battle, aware of the fact that no matter what outlandish performance the devil had planned for me that particular weekend. The Lord had gone a step ahead of him. Again, He spoke saying, "If he taunts you, taunt him back." Now whenever "'ole slewfoot" comes a callin', I simply remind him of his defeat according to the word of God and with it, this little tune:

"Okay, ya'll, here's to calling those things that be not yet; as though they are. Come on sing along, you know the song: "Ding dong, the prince is dead. Which old prince? The wicked prince! Ding, dong, the wicked prince is dead. Wake up, you sleepy head, rub your eyes; get out of bed. Wake up, the wicked prince is dead! He's gone where the goblins go below, below, below; yo-ho, let's open up and sing and ring the bells out: Ding-dong, the merry-o! Sing it high, sing it low; let them know the wicked prince is dead."

Point of Contact

Do not try debating with the devil; you will only end up in a state of confusion. Besides, he is a master of disguises. Try this: remind him of the day Christ died; I cannot explain it, but that seems to get right under his skin.

Chapter Three

Dating

*M*y son, if thou wilt receive my words, and hide my commandments with thee; so that thou incline thine ear unto wisdom, and apply thine heart to understanding. Yea, if thou criest after knowledge and liftest up thy voice for understanding; if thou seekest her as silver, and searchest for her as for hid treasures; Then shalt thou understand the fear of the Lord, and the knowledge of God (Prov. 2:1-5).*

Trust in the Lord with all thine heart, and lean not unto thine own understanding. In all thy ways acknowledge Him, and He shall direct thy paths (Prov. 3:5-6).

But they that wait upon the Lord shall renew their strength; they shall mount up with wings as eagles; they shall run, and not be weary; and they shall walk, and not faint (Is. 40:31).

Missing Out

To every thing there is a season, and a time to every purpose under the heaven (Eccl. 3:1).

As girls growing up in my parents' home, the thought of dating the opposite sex or doing anything prematurely was as forbidden to my three sisters and myself as the tree of knowledge was to Adam and Eve. No doubt, my parents loved us and wanted to preserve us for a much higher call, without any interruptions.

But, as the years quickly rolled by, the thrill of playing hopscotch and dolls seemed foolish and pointless. Our impression of fulfillment had a meaning all its own that did not include my parents' viewpoint on such matters. So, for some time, we struggled with what is known as "missing out." For teenage girls, the thought of being spectators in the arena of life was as frustrating as a basketball player always showing up for practice, but never given a chance to participate in a game. Therefore, for a short time, there was no small talk throughout the house concerning our feeling on the matter.

My mom, suddenly being aware of the changes that had taken place in us, knew that there was only one thing to do and that was to let go, and let God. Naturally speaking this did not happen without some struggle on her part. I mean, come on, what's a mother to do? After all, to hold on to something so much could mean losing it anyway, so why not turn it loose and into the hands of the One who created it to start with. So without further delay and without abandoning her duty as representative over the lives that God had given her to guard, she released us, and then affectionately said, "You're not missing out on anything, I promise!"

I didn't understand that then, because frustration had taken over, and my raging hormones were of no help. However, later on in life – even after the absence of my mother – while standing on a friend's balcony, I realized that everything did have its own season, and everything I sought to enjoy would all happen in its own time; I really had not missed anything.

For you young people with listening ears, God has an appointed time for everything that you are to do in this life; yes, fun is included. I know that this sounds mind-boggling to the young, and the young at heart, but it's true, and if you give Him all that you are right where you are, some incredibly wonderful things will happen to you.

Point of Contact

Consider group dating, and feel free to ask a sibling or cousin along with you for the ride. However, focus on dreams and goals and, ask God to allow you to bring them to pass.

Divorce

Whosoever shall put away his wife, saving for the cause of fornication, causeth her to commit adultery: and whosoever shall marry her that is divorced committeth adultery (Mt. 5:32).

Show me Thy ways, O Lord; teach me Thy paths. Lead me in Thy truth: and teach me: for Thou art the God of my salvation; on Thee do I wait all the day (Ps. 25:4-5).

I will instruct thee and teach thee in the way which thou shalt go: I will guide thee with Mine eye (Ps. 32:8).

O send out Thy light and Thy truth: let them lead me; let them bring me unto Thy holy hill, and to Thy tabernacles. Then will I go unto the altar of God, unto God my exceeding joy; yea, upon the harp will I praise Thee, O God my God (Ps. 43:3-4).

Peace I leave with you, My peace, I give unto you: not as the world giveth, give I unto you. Let not your heart be troubled, neither let it be afraid (Jn. 14:27).

If we say that we have fellowship with Him and walk in darkness, we lie, and do not the truth: But if we walk in the light, as He is in the light, we have fellowship one with another and the blood of Jesus Christ His Son cleanseth us from all sin (1 Jn. 1:6-7).

Light and Darkness

Be ye not unequally yoked together with unbelievers: for what fellowship hath righteousness with unrighteousness? And what communion hath light with darkness? (2 Cor. 6:14).

Divorce in America has become such a casual event that the enemy is, no doubt, having a field day at our expense. We Christians, and non-Christians alike, have become victims in the battle of the sexes, while a spirit of division plays the dictator.

A passerby shared a story with me concerning a young man and his fiancée. He said, "There was a young man, a born again believer, who suddenly discovered that his fiancée was not born again. Though their interest in most things was compatible, she did not share his interest in the Lord. Soon, the young man inquired of the Lord that he might arrive at a proper decision before his wedding day but not long afterwards the Lord spoke to him saying, "How can light live with darkness?" At that moment, the young man, though disappointed, made a decision not to marry her. Later, after sharing this news with his fiancée, the two of them cried on each others shoulder, and then parted, each going their own separate ways."

The moral of this story is that, the Spirit of God who dwells on the inside of you as a believer will separate you from the darkness that overshadows an unbeliever. Therefore, the joy that was intended for you as a couple in Christ, may be prolonged or shattered.

Point of Contact

Consider writing out a plan for your next move; perhaps going back to school, changing careers, or just pampering yourself; these are just a few of the things we can do to pick ourselves up and begin again. At all cost, be determined not to make your bed in limbo. Remember that God is the only one who promised never to leave or forsake us (Heb. 13:5).

Marriage

And be ye kind one to another, tender hearted, forgiving one another, even as God for Christ's sake hath forgiven you (Eph. 4:32).

Wives submit yourselves unto your own husbands, as unto the Lord. For the husband is the head of the wife, even as Christ is the Head of the Church: and He is Savior of the body. Husbands, love your wives, even as Christ also loved the Church, and gave Himself for it (Eph. 5:22-23, 25).

For even hereunto were ye called: because Christ also suffered for us, leaving us an example, that ye should follow His steps: Who did no sin, neither was guile found in His mouth: Who, when He was reviled, reviled not again; when He suffered, He threatened not; but committed Himself to Him that judgeth righteously.... Likewise, ye wives, be in subjection to your own husbands; that, if any obey not the Word, they also may without the Word be won by the conversation of the wives; while they behold your chaste conversation coupled with fear.... Likewise, ye husbands, dwell with them according to knowledge, giving honour unto the wife, as unto the weaker vessel, and as being heirs together of the grace of life; that your prayers be not hindered. Finally, be of one mind, having compassion one of another...be merciful, be courteous: Not rendering evil for evil, or railing for railing: but contrariwise blessing; knowing that ye are thereunto called, that ye should inherit a blessing (1 Pet. 2:21-23; 3:1-2, 7-9.

Here Comes the Bride

We then that are strong, ought to bear the infirmities of the weak, and not to please ourselves. Let everyone of us please his [spouse] for his good to edification (Rom. 15:1-2).

In a world where there's such indifference to the things we hold so beloved and so treasured and where sacred things are honored less and less, the purpose for marriage and the church's existence remains so clear: Together, you and I, we are the bride of Christ.

My, isn't she lovely? Family and friends express sentiments of delight to one another as the bride walked down the aisle, all dolled up. A vision of loveliness adorned in an ivory colored, full length, lace gown, with a silk taffeta train. On her head was a tiara of marquisette ornaments, accented with pearls, and fittingly attached was a silk tier veil that hung about mid-section. The groom stood there handsomely decked out in a full, dark, dress tailcoat with satin pockets and satin covered buttons; he appeared calm yet ready to go, that he might take his bride in arms and the two of them begin their wonderful new life together. Standing there, arm in arm, in the midst of family, friends, and God, the two vowed to cherish, honor and love one another through all of life's many difficulties.

The Rain

Five years later, the bride who once vowed "for better or worse" packed her bags, declaring their irreconcilable differences. The husband also agreed to the permanent arrangement, and the two made a decision to call it quits. What happened? Where did they go wrong? Did they fail to recognize that one person's shortcoming could very well be the other's strength? Or perhaps, what one considers a downside, the other might very well find it to be the thing that ties the marriage together for a perfect union.

Check this out

No two persons are completely compatible – we are just not designed that way. However, if we can understand our own weaknesses as well as our strengths, perhaps we may begin to view marriage in a completely new light.

Point of Contact

Guard your relationship in marriage, as you would the pupil of your eye.

———————

Singleness

A man that hath friends must show himself friendly (Prov. 18:24).

But seek ye first the Kingdom of God, and His righteousness; and all these things shall be added unto you (Mt. 6:33).

Hast thou faith? Have it to thyself before God (Rom. 14:22).

For ye have need of patience, that, after ye have done the will of God, ye might receive the promise (Heb. 10:36).

Knowing this, that the trying of your faith worketh patience (Jas. 1:3).

If any of you lack wisdom, let him ask of God, that giveth to all men liberally, and upbraided not; and it shall be given him (Jas. 1:5).

But every man hath his proper gift of God, one after this manner, and another after that (1 Cor. 7:7).

But I would have you without carefulness. He that is unmarried careth for the things that belong to the Lord, how he may please the Lord (1 Cor. 7:32).

I Gotta Man

Do you suppose that when Mary of Magdalene met Jesus, she suddenly met her first love? No doubt, Mary had known quite a few men in her occupation, but meeting Jesus was a different feeling of love than the love to which she had grown accustomed. Upon meeting Jesus, she felt loved! Her appearance and credentials, not even her present occupation made any difference to Him, whatsoever. I would imagine what he saw in Mary was a lonely, bewildered soul who needed to know that she was loved unconditionally.

One day, a co-worker shared her feelings of despair with me on being single and lonely. "Girl," she said, "I feel so alone and unaccepted; everyone I know is married, and I would love to share my life with someone who loves me, and I them."

"But, well, let me put it this way," she continued, "No one's knocking down my door for a chance to get to know me, let alone put a ring on my finger... and that's frightening." She went on, "It seems as though I will never meet Mr. Right, and girl, I hear that old 'bio' clock tickin'."

She seemed depressed, as though at some time in her life, someone said, "marry, or die!" I stared at her for a few seconds and tried to think of encouraging words to say; anything to help her get through her day without looking so downcast. Therefore, I threw a couple of jokes her way hoping to at least put a smirk on her face; but there was no smile, and after my busy morning on the job, I was drained. Her fear of being single and alone went beyond fruitless words.

I have a tendency of being a burden bearer whenever a matter of the heart presents itself. This is something God knows well about me, and therefore, every now and then (not always), He allows me the privilege of practical exercise in the field of a given situation. Whenever my workday ended, I carried this woman's emotional distress home with me that I might turn it over to the Lord in prayer, on her behalf. Now, I'm no counselor, but the Holy Spirit is, and although I didn't have a clue as to how I might be of any help to her, He assured me that God had a plan and purpose for her present state in life.

That evening, while alone in my kitchen, the Spirit of God impressed these words on my heart, "Tell her to allow Jesus her husbandman, that He might show her the way to wholeness." He continued, "Tell her, you know the way." Several days later, I shared this news with my co-worker and she was amazed. Actually, according to her, this was a confirmation. She informed me that her Pastor who counseled her several days earlier shared the same message to her. She was overjoyed just to think that God loved her so much that He would help her prepare for whatever the future held.

On Being Single

I wish I knew then what I know now because there is so much to know. Marriage, like anything else, is hard work and if you think that you can do it without God's help, especially in this day and time, you're fooling yourself. There are so many hurdles to leap over and after a while, you lose count of how many you have faced. However, marriage is a beautiful thing when you allow God to prepare you for it beforehand.

Here are a few advantages of being single, while preparing for marriage:

- Being single will allow you to develop a deeper relationship with your Creator.
- Being single can help you manage your money sensibly.

- Being single will allow you to enjoy yourself, and know what makes you happy.
- Being single can help you identify what real love is.
- Being single will allow you to identify your strengths and weaknesses beforehand.
- Being single can help you make smart decisions, and make them count.
- Being single can help you identify what you want and do not want in a husband.
- Being single will enable you to spend time in prayer concerning the husband that God has chosen for you.
- Being single will enable you to focus on being a godly mother.
- Being single will enable you to be confident about you, the person God created.

Here Comes the Bride!

I gotta a Man; He is like no other,
He cares for me better than a father, a mother, a lover.
When I turn the key, I know He'll be there,
Ready to greet me, even with wind blown hair.
My makeup's a mess, but He doesn't care,
I'm amazed at how much He's willing to share.
Yea, I got a Man; this I won't deny,
Don't have to worry either, 'bout Him making me cry.
When nighttime falls, I know I'm in good hands,
Yea, I'm doin' alright ya'll, 'cause I got a Man.

Point of Contact

Giving one's self a marital deadline will only keep you in bondage; not to mention, it will stress you to tears. Learn how to celebrate the "you" that God created. Take yourself out to dinner, buy yourself flowers (especially on Valentine's Day), or write a poem to yourself about the person God has created you to be. Last, but not least: don't be anxious. Wait on God. The time you spend in planning, praying and preparing will be well worth it.

Chapter Four

Angels

*T*hen the woman came and told her husband, saying, A man of God came unto me, and His countenance was like the countenance of an angel of God, very terrible: but I asked Him not whence he was, neither told He me His name (Judg. 13:6).

The angel of the Lord encampeth round about them that fear Him, and delivereth them (Ps. 34:7).

For He shall give His angels charge over thee, to keep thee in all thy ways. They shall bear thee up in their hands, lest thou dash thy foot against a stone (Ps. 91:11-12).

Bless ye the Lord, all ye His hosts; ye ministers of His, that do His pleasure (Ps. 103:20).

My God hath sent His angel, and hath shut the lions' mouths, that they have not hurt me (Dan. 6:22).

Angels Unaware

Are they not all ministering spirits, sent forth to minister for them who shall be heirs of salvation? (Heb. 1:14)

How would you like to see the person standing next to you in a new and unmistakable light? Perhaps you've never seen an angel before – not one dressed up in heavenly garments – but perhaps through the kindness of a stranger, or maybe a person dressed in tattered clothing with a smile that brightened your day. It is written: "Be not forgetful to entertain strangers: for thereby some have entertained angels unawares" (Heb. 13:2).

A couple of months before the birth of my son, who was delivered prematurely through cesarean section, the Lord impressed upon my heart preparations of an early delivery. I was certain that through prayer, God would allow me more time, but time would not have benefited the outcome. Within a couple of weeks, my doctor informed me that nothing further could be done to prolong my pregnancy – my son must be delivered right then. I'd like to say that my faith doubled the size of a mustard seed, but faith was not present; there was only fear. The kind of fear that makes you feel helpless and discouraged.

Although I knew of God's word, I'd given little or no time to it so I could not recall any of the promises in my time of need. And, these were the promises that would assure me of God's love and His presence when facing dark, uncertain moments. But, thanks unto God for He is faithful even when we are not: Hallelujah!

There I stood in that little room alone, with tears streaming down my face, scared, nervous and worried. When suddenly, this person walked up to me and smiled. I stared at her for moment, knowing that she was not the nurse assigned to me as a patient, nor had I seen her at any time during my previous days there. But there she stood in a white nurse's uniform with a little white hat that I didn't realize nurses wore still. Honestly, her smile was like that of a beautiful child and her apparent movement was graceful. Suddenly, she spoke saying, "Don't worry, everything will be alright!" With this, she explained the entire procedure involving the surgery, and timed it precisely; I didn't say a word, because the confidence in her voice gave me hope.

Just then, I turned my head to make sure a chair was directly behind that I might sit down, and then turned towards her to thank her, but she was gone. Naturally, I did not give it much thought then because of the joyful event that took place afterward; but even to this day, I cannot forget the face of that beautiful being dressed up in a nurse's uniform. Have you been visited by an angel lately?

Point of Contact

Your angel stands in the very presence of God waiting to be activated by you.

God

In the beginning God created the heaven and the earth (Gen. 1:1).

The Lord is a man of war... (Ex. 15:3).

...Thou art a gracious and merciful God (Neh. 9:31).

O taste and see that the Lord is good.... (Ps. 34:8).

The Mighty God...hath spoken (Ps. 50:1).

Unto thee, O God, do we give thanks...for that Thy Name is near Thy wondrous works declare (Ps. 75:1).

Behold, God is my salvation... (Is. 12:2).

Our Father which art in heaven... (Mt. 6:9).

O the depth of the riches both of the wisdom and knowledge of God! How unsearchable are His judgments, and His ways past finding out! (Rom.11:33).

...The King of kings (1 Tim. 6:15).

Draw nigh to God, and He will draw nigh to you (Jas. 4:8).

God is love... (1 Jn. 4:16).

Our Father

TO THE UNKNOWN GOD: Whom therefore ye ignorantly worship, Him declare I unto you (Acts 17:23).

Do you ever think about God, the Father? You know, the Ancient of Days. Have you ever imagined Him as I have with a flowing white robe and wooly white hair, standing mightily with a bullwhip? Do you see Him documenting our every move ready to discipline us whenever we step out of line with a finger pointed in our direction saying, "Don't play with me, I've taken your foolishness long enough." You may be wondering, "How could you say such a thing?" But let me tell you, the devil has wasted no time in suggesting these very same thoughts about God to most of us, hoping to get us to rebel against Him; no doubt he's been very busy and very successful, don't you think?

You know, back in the day, I thought God was simply an old man who lived in ancient times. One whom had fallen into a deep sleep and, through the passing of time, dreamed of a world much like this one where we as humans here on earth were the result of His dream in operation. I simply could not allow myself to accept the fact that any one being had no beginning and no end. But, one evening, some years later, I sat down and asked the Holy Spirit to reveal the Father to me in a way that I might understand. Immediately, I began to think of my dad, who was deceased, yet my thoughts centered on his presence when we were together as a family. His presence brought balance and a sense of security in our home.

After a little while, the Spirit of God revealed my heavenly Father to me, as I began to recite the "Our father" in the Lord 's Prayer. The moment I said those words, a divine presence enveloped me and a wonderful peace filled my soul. I looked up and whispered the word "Daddy." No longer did I see Him as someone distant, holding a bullwhip, or even as an old man from ancient times with a vivid dream. But, a very loving Father who wanted to put his arms around me and let me know that everything would be alright. Tears stream my face as I thought to myself, "God, my Father really loves me! He loves us all, and He will love us throughout all eternity. 'For we are also His offspring'" (Acts 17:28).

Point of Contact

Spend a few minutes each day reading God's Word, then ask the Spirit of the God to reveal your Father to you in a way that you might understand and worship Him.

Holy Spirit

In the beginning...the Spirit of God moved upon the face of the waters. (Gen. 1:2).

...The Holy Ghost...shall teach you all things, and bring all things to your remembrance (Jn. 14:26).

...The Spirit of truth...will guide you into all truth (Jn. 16:13).

But ye shall receive power, after that the Holy Ghost is come upon you: and ye shall be witnesses unto Me... (Acts 1:8).

...His Spirit...dwelleth in you (Rom. 8:11).

...Being sanctified by the Holy Ghost (Rom. 15:16).

But God hath revealed them unto us by His Spirit (1 Cor. 2:10).

...According to His mercy He saved us, by the washing of regeneration, and renewing of the Holy Ghost (Titus 3:5).

Like the Wind

The wind blows wherever it pleases. You hear its sound, but you cannot tell where it comes from or where it is going (Jn. 3:8).

When I was growing up, there was very little emphasis concerning God's Spirit. It was as though He were an old godly man, perhaps a monk, a do-gooder, who cared for the poor and little children with severe illnesses. Why, even during my catechism classes, he remained the silent Person of the Trinity. So instead of relating to Him as God – the third person, we honored the mother of God, placing her in high esteem – a sort of forerunner to Christ.

Surely, I am not suggesting that Mary be forgotten for her submission to God; after all, it was through her obedience that Christ came to us, and through Him the salvation of our souls. But, little, if anything, was made known concerning the fact that God's Spirit is the one who guides us throughout this journey and invites us to be God-chasers. Because this knowledge was never presented in our hearing, it was easy to link Him to a beautiful dove in order that a name and an entity might come together to satisfy the shallow thinking of man.

Back in the day, we'd gather together – my mother, sisters, and myself around the kitchen table in prayer – recalling the needs of the family and simply to spend time in God's presence. What a wonderful season to remember! But even more wonderful was God's Spirit who revealed His presence, by way of a gentle breeze throughout our kitchen. My mother recognizing His presence would then say, "He's here! Ask Him to present your needs to the Father." I didn't understand what she meant whenever she'd say, "He's here!" You see, I understood God as Father and I thought I knew enough about God the Son, but I could not understand the title – the position of this third Person of the Trinity.

However, early one morning and about a few pages away from completing this manuscript, this question was presented to me: "Now what type of audience do you suppose would benefit from your book?" Why those with listening ears, I suggested. But then, a very gentle voice spoke up on the inside of me and said: "Even Paul's messages were not for the benefit of Paul alone or those with listening ears." The voice continued, "I move according to the plan and purpose of God and to put limits on Me would be like trying to box the wind, and you cannot box the wind." I smiled, and thanked God for the presence of His Spirit – this third person of the trinity, the wind of God.

Point of Contact

Holy Spirit, make me sensitive to Your still, small voice.

———————

Jesus

And His Name shall be called...The mighty God... (Is. 9:6).

...Even the unclean spirits...do obey Him (Mk. 1:27).

The Holy Ghost shall come upon thee, and...that Holy Thing which shall be born of thee shall be called the Son of God (Lk. 1:35).

In the beginning was the Word, and the Word was with God, and the Word was God.... And the Word was made flesh, and dwelt among us (Jn. 1:1 & 14).

Jesus saith unto him, "I am the way, the truth, and the life: no man cometh unto the Father, but by Me" (Jn. 14:6).

...Whom God hath raised from the dead (Acts 3:15).

...In every thing ye are enriched by Him, in all utterance, and in all knowledge.... Christ the power of God, and the wisdom of God (1 Cor. 1:5 & 24).

...He abideth faithful.... (2 Tim. 2:13).

Jesus, the Legend

In the beginning was the Word, and the Word was with God, and the Word was God (Jn. 1:1).

Why do you suppose that Jesus, the Son of God was the most talked about, acclaimed, yet reviled Person on the face of this earth, even today? Even during His earthly existence why do you suppose demons, even Satan himself feared Him? I'll cut to the chase and say what I believe. It was because Jesus lived God's Word. Let's face it, most people find it difficult to take a stand for those things that are honest and true, and find it even more complicated to speak the word of God in the face of temptations and trials. Overall, most of us find it difficult simply to stand our ground where our integrity is concerned.

But, you know, I don't think that Jesus overcame temptation in the desert, or the many trials in His life, or anything else for that matter, simply because He was the Son of God. And, no! He didn't walk around with a halo of light over His head, warding off demonic attack to gain the upper hand. He knew who He was, and whose He was, and the Word was with Him, in Him... He *is* the Word.

Jesus – the legend lives on!

Point of Contact

Even if you are not feelin' Jesus, do not deny yourself the privilege of knowing Him. Ask the Holy Spirit to reveal the unseen Christ to you, that you might begin to "feel" Him.

Chapter Five

Family

*N*ow the LORD hath said unto Abram, Get thee out of thy country, and from thy kindred, and from thy father's house, unto a land that I will show thee (Gen. 12:1).

God setteth the solitary in families: He bringeth out those which are bound with chains: but the rebellious dwell in a dry land (Ps. 68:6).

Behold, how good and how pleasant it is for brethren to dwell together in unity! (Ps. 133:1).

He that trouble his own house shall inherit the wind: and the fool shall be servant to the wise of heart (Prov. 11:29).

Roots

My mother and My brethren are these which hear the word of God, and do it (Lk. 8:21).

"I must be about My Father's business!" Sounds pretty deep. Especially, where family members and family traditions are concerned. Although our love for one another should enable us to go from glory to glory with the help of the Spirit, sometimes ungodly soul-ties wrap cords around our mind, preventing us from moving according to God's plan for us, individually.

My Uncle officiated my wedding ceremony, a priest in our family; his message was clear to those with listening ears. Briefly, he said, "Individuals, as well as couples, should be given room to grow and spread their wings, even if it seems out of line with family traditions." That message came in loud and clear to me then, and it is especially clear now. You see, God's call on an individual's life is personal and precious; therefore, this call may not coincide with the thoughts and plans of those who do not understand God's ways.

Those ungodly soul ties may very well prevent you from fulfilling God's call on your life. Therefore love your family in Christ and realize, like Jesus, that you must be about your Father's business (Lk. 2:49).

Point of Contact

After one time comes another! Laugh with one another, love each other, and share your memories. Nevertheless, understand that God designed each and every one of us for a specific purpose, that which may separate us from the family circle. Choose to let go, and let God.

Generational Curses

Let the redeemed of the Lord say so, whom He hath redeemed from the hand of the enemy; And gathered them out of the lands, from the east, and from the west, from the north, and from the south (Ps. 107:1-3).

But as many as received Him, to them gave He power to become the sons of God, even to them that believe on His Name (Jn. 1:12).

If the Son therefore shall make you free, ye shall be free indeed (Jn. 8:36).

For the law of the Spirit of life in Christ Jesus hath made me free from the law of sin and death (Rom. 8:2).

Be not deceived: evil communications corrupt good manners (1 Cor. 15:33).

Therefore, if any man be in Christ, he is a new creature: old things are passed away; behold, all things are become new (2 Cor. 5:17).

Christ hath redeemed us from the curse of the law, being made a curse for us: for it is written, cursed is every one that hangeth on a tree: that the blessing of Abraham might come on the Gentiles through Jesus Christ; that we might receive the promise of the Spirit through faith (Gal. 3:13-14).

Black Sheep

The fathers have eaten sour grapes, and the children's teeth are set on edge? (Ez. 18:2).

Baa, baa, black sheep, have you any wool? Yes sir, yes sir, three bags full....

So you're the black sheep of the family? Well, don't worry about it! After all, we've all picked up a vice-like grip from our ancestors, perhaps as far back as the fourth generation, maybe even farther than that. But, wait a minute! "What exactly are generational curses?"

Strongholds, I say! You know, those things that are not easily shaken.

Though unwanted, still you can't do anything about flaws that show and put a damper on your already not so perfect character; something that was handed down to you without request from your old Aunt Bev on your father's side. "You know an apple never falls that far from the tree," that's what the folks used to say.

When I was growing up, the folks use to say, "O, that child is something else – but he didn't steal it you know!" In other words, that child's habits or behavioral pattern was simply a repetition of one parent or the other, or perhaps someone else on the family tree. So, after hearing it over and over again, the poor kid grew up repeating the same behavioral pattern of his forerunner.

Indeed there are many shortcomings still hanging on a limb on my family tree, or bag's of wool, as I call them. Things that have attached themselves to me and I to them, as though inseparable. But, the good news is I don't have to live under those curses. No, because the law of the Spirit of life in Christ Jesus hath made me free from the law of sin and death (Rom. 8:2).

Therefore, I am free from those old chains that had me bound and I can freely walk in my generational blessings.

Point of Contact

The Word of God says, if we decree a thing, it shall be so (Job 22:28). Therefore, declare every generational curse broken in Jesus' Name, and acknowledge your generational blessings.

Unity

Depart from evil, and do good; seek peace, and pursue it (Ps. 34:14).

The eyes of the Lord are upon the righteous, and His ears are open unto their cry (Ps. 34:15).

Behold, how good and how pleasant it is for brethren to dwell together in unity! (Ps. 133:1).

Again I say unto you, that if two of you shall agree on earth as touching any thing that they shall ask, it shall be done for them of my Father, which is in heaven (Mt. 18:19).

Let love be without dissimulation, abhor that which is evil; cleave to that which is good (Rom. 12:9).

Now I beseech you, brethren, by the Name of our Lord Jesus Christ, that ye all speak the same thing, and that there be no division among you; but that ye be perfectly joined together in the same mind and in the same judgment (1 Cor. 1:10).

Coat of Many Colors

Every kingdom divided against itself is brought to desolation, and every city or house divided against itself shall not stand (Mt. 12:25).

Whether home, social group, city, kingdom, or the body of Christ, unity is vital in the direction of growth and well-being. Division, on the other hand, retards the growth process and destroys progression. It is like that of deadly venom making its way towards destruction. Surely, those who are called to be leaders have experienced its self-centered purpose at some point in their lives.

Every family has a leader: someone who is able to hold things together and lead. A leader has the gift of influencing others. They are usually outspoken, or at least unafraid to take a stand. Their willingness to take the initiative, even if they must go at it alone, enables them to tear down walls that ordinarily would never come down, preparing the way for the next stage.

Indeed, there are different types of leaders, however, one called upon to assume responsibility for the way of peace is a leader after God's own heart. Those who are called into leadership understand that order plays a vital role in helping to bring stability and wholeness in any situation.

In my own family, unity was never really one of our strong attributes. I would imagine the enemy, the devil, lured his way in when no one was watching (with spiritual eyes) and snatched it away before it had a chance to take root. Even so, unity flowing together with harmony must begin someplace, and in order for it to take root, one must make it a passionate thing.

My in-laws on the other hand were blessed with unity among themselves, and though it does not appear to be God-given to them, they are consistent at making it a guiding force in their lives. It is written: "Indeed, when Gentiles, who do not have the law, do by nature things required by the law, they are a law for themselves, even though they do not have the law, since they show that the requirements of the law are written on their hearts (Rom. 2:14-15).

Point of Contact

Since we all operate with different gifts, make a note of each individual's potential gift and ask them to operate in that position; don't forget to let every voice be heard so that peace reigns. Finally, keep in mind that no one really appreciates a "know-it-all."

Chapter Six

His Good Fight

A poem that defeated a wicked spirit
during the midnight hour

One night as I lay in bed asleep, I envisioned a hideous creature dressed in a black cape with a hood on his head staring at me. He stood there holding a book of some kind, and angrily stared at me as though I had something to offer him. Immediately (in the spirit), I began to plead the blood of Jesus, but he was stubborn and refused to leave. Just then, while asleep, somewhere in my subconscious mind, I uttered these words:

Do you remember the Man who died on the cross?
His Name was Jesus, the Christ.
God's Holy Son who came down from heaven,
To put the enemy to flight.

Born of a virgin, through the power of God's Spirit,
The anointed One was He.
He went about healing, loving and caring,
To set all captives free:

With twelve-band of men, better known as disciples,
He invaded the enemy's camp.
So, one of them was used of you Satan;
But, not even that stopped the champ.

In three years' time, He shook the earth,
With the power of God's might.
This He did in three short years,
To show us how to fight the good fight!

Authority

Verily I say unto you, whatsoever ye shall bind on earth shall be bound in heaven: and whatsoever ye shall loose on earth shall be loosed in heaven (Mt. 18:18).

For though we walk in the flesh, we do not war after the flesh: For the weapons of our warfare are not carnal, but mighty through God to the pulling down of strong holds (2 Cor. 10:3-4).

Casting down imaginations, and every high thing that exalteth itself against the knowledge of God, and bringing into captivity every thought to the obedience of Christ; and having in a readiness to revenge all disobedience, when your obedience is fulfilled (Cor. 10:5-6).

And hath raised us up together, and made us sit in heavenly places in Christ Jesus (Eph. 2:6).

Put on the whole armour of God, that ye may be able to stand against the wiles of the devil. For we wrestle not against flesh and blood, but against principalities, against powers, against the rulers of the darkness of this world, against spiritual wickedness in high places (Eph. 6:12).

Wanna Be Startin' Somethin'

Were you there when they crucified my Lord? Were you there when they crucified my Lord? O, sometimes, it causes me to tremble, tremble, tremble. Were you there when they crucified my Lord?

...Even the devils are subject unto us through Thy Name: And He said unto them, I beheld Satan as lighting fall from heaven. Behold, I give unto you power to tread on serpents and scorpions, and over all the power of the enemy: and nothing shall by any means hurt you (Lk. 10:17-18-19).

If fighting the good fight against a person of flesh and blood causes you to falter, how will you do battle against your great enemy, the devil, and be victorious? I've often wondered how could a loving, all-knowing God stand aloof while the enemy, Satan, wreaks havoc throughout the earth. I used to ask myself, "Doesn't he know what's going on, or does He care?" People killing one another, stealing, abusing – my, Satan's busy!

One day, during what I recognized as an attack from the enemy, I paused in the middle of my prayers and asked the Lord this question, "Can't you do something? Won't you even stop him from his vicious attacks? He's getting a kick out of it, I'm quite sure." It did appear as though the Lord was not listening, but later that evening after reading Luke chapter 22, I began to meditate on that entire event.

Narrator: It was piercing cold, unlike any other night during this time of year.

Hell's Raiders: This is it ya'll, he's goin' down.

Satan: Yea! The verdict has been pronounced; he's as good as dead.

The Council: Tell us! Art Thou the Christ?

Jesus: Ye say that I am. Hereafter shall the Son of Man sit on the right hand of the power of God (Lk. 22:69-70).

Pilot: I will therefore chastise Him, and release Him.

Narrator: But they cried saying, crucify Him, crucify Him. Upon Pilate's release of the spotless Lamb, He was taken away and led down the road to Calvary.

Narrator: While hanging on the cross, He cried out.

Jesus: Father, forgive them, for they know not what they do (Lk. 23:34).

Narrator: Then, from about the sixth to the ninth hour, the earth became as black as midnight, and the sun was darkened, and the veil of the temple was torn apart. Suddenly, He cried again saying...

Jesus: Father, into Thy hands I commend My Spirit, and He died (Lk. 23:44-46).

Narrator: Now upon the first day of the week, very early in the morning, the stone where King Jesus laid to rest, was rolled away from the sepulcher (Lk. 24:1-2). Not long after this, He went back to the Father; He was manifested that He might destroy the works of the devil (1 Jn. 3:8).

That night, it dawned on me that my authority over the devil is simply knowing that Jesus suffered and died that I might have authority over him.

Point of Contact

If only we knew half of what the devil knows about us and more about our position in Christ, we'd jump out of bed in the morning with a grin, saying, "C'mon, make my day."

Power

Drink ye all of it; for this is My blood of the new testament, which is shed for many for the remission of sins (Mt. 26:28).

Whom God hath set forth to be a propitiation through faith in His blood, to declare His righteousness for the remission of sins that are past, through the forbearance of God (Rom. 3:25).

Having therefore, brethren, boldness to enter into the holiest by the blood of Jesus, by a new and living way, which He hath consecrated for us, through the veil, that is to say His flesh; and having an high priest over the house of God (Heb. 10:19-20).

This is He that came by water and blood, even Jesus Christ; not by water only, but by water and blood (1 Jn. 5:6).

The Lambs' Blood

And they overcame him by the blood of the Lamb, and by the word of their testimony (Rev. 12:1).

I've discovered that the blood of Jesus not only redeemed us, but protects us from the tricks and attacks of the enemy.

Very early one morning, I encountered a rather disturbing situation on the job. A woman approached me who was obviously under the influence of alcohol, the devil's power of suggestion, and God only knows what else. At first she appeared to be sober and sound, but in a split second she went into a furious rage with all sorts of profanity coming out of her mouth. I must admit I was a little disturbed, to say the least.

There we were together in an office about the size of my dress closet, with her starring at me ill at ease, as though I reminded her of an unusual dream. I too felt nervous, because it's not every day that you encounter one's soul breathing down your neck in a stuffy little room with unfitted furniture. Besides that, there appeared to be no way out and, as it was, she stood in the doorway as if deliberately trying to block my pathway.

Let me just say that the fact that she was stoned was not a bother to me; I could have dealt with that. But there appeared to be a kind of rage in her that I discerned as demonic. A little while later, she boldly claimed that she was the devil. I pretended to be calm, but inside I shook like a dried leaf on a tree. Look, this did not occur at two in the afternoon, but rather at two in the wee hours of the morning; imagine that! As I stood still in that little cramped up office, I recall asking the Lord this question: Why me? Then almost without thinking, He answered through me. Let's face it, rarely will the devil bother you if you pose no threat to his way of operation.

She stood there staring at me disapprovingly, with glassy eyes, as if waiting for me to make a move that she might leap on me and tear me to shreds. Right then, I began to pray, asking the Lord for divine help. Suddenly, I heard a voice speak up on the inside saying, "Quick use your weapon." Just then I was reminded of the power in the blood of Jesus. At that moment, I began to plead the blood over self, this woman, and the author of evil.

Strangely enough, not long afterward, the woman fell backwards and began calling on the Name of Jesus.

Later, though it was obvious that she was still under the influence of alcohol, I was able to lead her to the door in peace; then at once, she turned to me, thanked me and gave me a great big hug.

The blood of Jesus will never lose its power.

Point of Contact

Since it is relatively impossible to avoid bumping into people who may be involved in occultism or any other form of satanic practices (this includes persons who unknowingly do so), cover yourself and your family with the blood of Jesus.

Chapter Seven

Death

*D*eath is swallowed up in victory. O death, where is thy sting? O grave, where is thy victory? (1 Cor. 15:55)

Since the children have flesh and blood, He too shared in their humanity so that by His death He might destroy him who holds the power of death – that is, the devil – and free those who all their lives were held in slavery by their fear of death (Heb. 2:14-15).

The Sting

Have you ever accused God for the death of a loved one, or perhaps death itself? I have! I thought that God could not wait for His children to leave this mortal existence and enter heaven's gates to become a member of His heavenly court; a sort of race against Satan to prove to us, His saints, that heaven is really a much better place.

Oh, I would imagine to most this sounds almost like blasphemy, but you'd be surprised at the many people who harbor feelings of bitterness against God, holding Him accountable for the death of a loved one.

Let's face it, death is something that we don't like to think about. On the contrary, most of us really don't want any part of it, not even to get to heaven. Huh! Whenever the "D-word" is mentioned, the majority of us – Christians and non-Christians alike – go into a state of panic, simply because our attachment to this earthly existence blinds us to what we cannot see or understand with our natural senses.

I'll never forget the day my mother told me about my dad's fatal illness and how much time he had left to be on this earth. She approached me after school one day and led me to our patio where she sat waiting to share the not so welcoming news – the bad report that she and my dad had received from his doctor. While standing there, I felt a pit at the bottom of my stomach as I listened in disbelief. This was not supposed to happen to us, we were not bad people.

Nevertheless, I tried my best to reason it all out as I walked away. You see, reasoning things out was one of my special assets and there was no time to lose. However, before I could come up with anything, my mom had it all figured out. We, as a family would turn to God in prayer and ask Him for a miracle. Not a "let's pray according to the word, because Jesus was bruised for our iniquities" kinda miracle, but your ordinary "religious" prayer kinda miracle.

Well, as time proceeded, my dad's condition seemed to be improving, but then suddenly it took a turn for the worse; unfortunately from there he was knocking at death's door. On a Thursday morning, at 10:25, during the month of June, my dad went home to be with the Lord. For me that was a sting like no other... the sting of death.

Since that time I've learned a very important lesson, and with it, my own little philosophy to get me through tough times.

Point of Contact

In life as we walk this Christian walk, we must learn to rely on God's promises if we hope to live a life of total abundance. Still, we must keep in mind that problems will follow. It is how we handle those problems, while relying on these promises, that we are able to share in the provision of this abundant life.

Grief

Weeping may endure for a night, but joy cometh in the morning (Ps. 30:5).

Blessed are they that mourn: for they shall be comforted (Mt. 5:4).

But I would not have you to be ignorant, brethren, concerning them which are asleep, that ye sorrow not, even as others which have no hope (1 Th. 4:13).

For if we believe that Jesus died and rose again, even so them also which sleep in Jesus will bring with Him. Wherefore comfort one another with these words (1 Th. 4:14-18).

Blessed be God, even the Father of our Lord Jesus Christ, the Father of mercies, and the God of all comfort; who comforted us in all our tribulation, that we may be able to comfort them which are in any trouble, by the comfort wherewith we ourselves are comforted of God (2 Cor. 1:3-4).

Beyond the Veil

Peace I leave with you, My peace I give unto you: not as the world giveth, give I unto you. Let not your heart be troubled, neither let it be afraid (Jn. 14:27).

There's a dark cloud that hangs over your head once you've laid a loved one to rest, and like a shadow it follows you around like an unwelcomed guest. Grief, like a dark tunnel of emotional distress brought on by a wound that only time, can heal in time. But let's face it! On our strength alone, the grief or sorrow that we feel from the passing of a loved one can be like an overwhelming nightmare; although a certain amount of grief is absolutely necessary. You must beware, however, for toying with it too long may send you into a sea of endless depression. My uncle once said, "Never dwell on that which causes sorrow, it only makes things worse and aborts the healing process." True, but the mind has a way of rewinding experiences for the sake of explanation.

One day while I was driving, I noticed how beautiful the day was so I complemented the Lord on His creativeness. For some reason my thoughts instantly turned to the day as it was, when my dad passed away. So many years had gone by and I still remembered that day and began reminiscing on the entire event. Before long, sorrow overwhelmed me, tears welled up in my eyes, and a spirit of self-pity began to wrap its weight around me, like that of a poisonous snake. However, before I descended any deeper into self-pity, the Lord gently rebuked me saying, "This day was presented for your enjoyment, why do you wish to bring a curse upon it?" Immediately, the Spirit of self-pity fled, and the peace of the Lord comforted me.

Truly, it is unnatural for us to think that we can avoid grief in this life. Why, the memories alone of that dear loved one will bring about a pain that cuts like a knife; but Jesus promised us a comforter, He is the Holy Spirit. I have felt His comforting arms whenever that cloud of gloom was present and have allowed His presence to take me beyond the veil.

Point of Contact

Comfort one another with words of peace. Also, allow a necessary amount of time and space for the healing of an open wound, or wounded heart. Finally, try to avoid those who are good at speaking before thinking.

Resurrection

For the hour is coming, in which all that are in the graves shall hear His voice, and shall come forth; they that have done good, unto the resurrection of life; and they that have done evil, unto the resurrection of damnation (Jn. 5:28-29).

For if we have been planted together in the likeness of His death, we shall be also in the likeness of His resurrection (Rom. 6:5).

And if Christ be not raised, your faith is vain; ye are yet in your sins. Then they also which are fallen asleep in Christ are perished (1 Cor. 15:17-18).

But now is Christ risen from the dead, and become the first fruit of them that slept (1 Cor. 15:20).

Behold, I show you a mystery; we shall not all sleep, but we shall
all be changed, in a moment; in the twinkling of an eye, at the last
trump: for the trumpet shall sound, and the dead shall be raised
incorruptible, and we shall be changed (1 Cor. 15:51-52).

Happy Resurrection Day

I am the resurrection, and the life: he that believeth in Me, though
he were dead, yet shall he live: Believest thou this? (Jn. 11:25-26).

She's gone – now what? After the passing of my mother, I grew a little
concerned over the whereabouts of her spirit. Her body, the empty shell that it
was, now displayed no hope of returning to its former existence. I was tempted
to doubt God's love that watches over His word for those who kept the faith.
So for weeks, I wrestled with thoughts that held me captive.

During the year that followed, on Good Friday, I decided to cry out to
God concerning the spirit of my mother. Oh I knew that she had a peace with
God and a relationship that was unique in every way. But, if I were going to
have any peace in this life concerning her death, and even desire to carry on
her faith legacy, I wanted to know that she was one of the chosen whose body
would one day be resurrected and caught up in the air as God's word declares.

It was early that Easter morning, while asleep, the Lord answered my
prayer request through a dream. In that dream, I saw my mother dressed in a
flowing white garment, with two angelic beings standing on either side of her,
the three of them stood in front of an oversized door inlayed with gold. This
dream continued long enough that I heard the Lord say:

I am the resurrection and the life: he that believeth in Me, though
he were dead, yet shall he live: And whosoever liveth and believeth
in Me shall never die (Jn. 11:25-26).

Point of Contact

If God said it, He will do it. If He spoke it, it's as good as done. Believe in
the resurrection.

Chapter Eight

Healing

O Lord my God, I cried unto Thee, and Thou hast healed me (Ps. 30:2).

Many are the afflictions of the righteous: but the Lord delivereth him out of them all (Ps. 34:19).

The Lord will strengthen him upon the bed of languishing: Thou wilt make all his bed in his sickness (Ps. 41:3).

My flesh and my heart faileth: but God is the strength of my heart, and my portion forever (Ps. 73:26).

Bless the Lord, O my soul, and forget not all His benefits: Who forgiveth all thine iniquities; who healeth all thy diseases; Who redeemeth thy life from destruction; who crowneth thee with loving kindness and tender mercies; Who satisfieth thy mouth with good things; so that thy youth is renewed like the eagle's (Ps. 103:2-5).

All Is Well

For I am the Lord that healeth thee (Ex. 15:26).

Do you need a healing from God? Perhaps, emotional, physical or mental? We all do at some time in our lives, some more often than others do. But, first we must believe that with God, nothing is impossible (Lk. 1:37).

Once upon a time, I was afraid to ask Jesus to heal me even of a sore thumb. Oh, I don't know, perhaps fear prevented me from doing so. Perhaps I was afraid that He would not really be listening unless I performed some type of religious ritual. Or maybe I just thought it best to identify suffering with martyrdom, assuming that the Lord would be pleased with such bondage. My doubt in God's ability to heal me, made it almost impossible for me to receive any type of healing.

Some years ago, I was diagnosed with endometriosis, an infirmity that attacks the uterine wall that caused me much pain in the lower abdomen and further caused normal tissues to grow in abnormal places. Well, like the woman with the issue of blood, I had spent time and money on doctors, but all to no avail. Then one day, the pain gripped me so until I could hardly stand it. Just then, I cried out to the Lord and He heard me. As I rose to my feet, the pain left my body completely in a way of slow motion; I was stunned, to say the least. Then the Lord spoke to my spirit saying, "My child, why have you waited so long to ask me to heal you?" Then He breathed the words of this song into my heart: "O what peace we often forfeit, O what needless pain we bare, all because we do not carry everything to God in prayer." I thank the Lord for His divine healing.

At times, it does seem that God isn't listening whenever we pray for healing. But, it is written, "Ask and ye shall receive, that your joy may be full" (Jn. 16:24). Hang on to the horns of the altar in faith; be willing to forgive everyone; repent of your sins, continue to confess your healing, seek wisdom and remember this:

With His stripes, we are healed (Isa. 53:5).

Point of Contact

The Bible says faith without works is dead (Jas. 2:26). Sometimes it helps to understand that the Lord will instruct us to seek medical help, and even natural remedies for our healing, while relying on his divine healing. What's more, keep in mind that there is nothing like the power of God's spoken word over any situation in your body or life. Be healed!

Hope

But Thou art He that took me out of the womb: Thou didst make me hope when I was upon my mother's breasts (Ps. 22:9).

Be of good courage, and He shall strengthen your heart, all ye that hope in the Lord (Ps. 31:24).

The Lord will perfect that which concerneth me: Thy mercy, O Lord, endureth forever: forsake not the works of Thine own hands (Ps. 138:8).

And we know that all things work together for good to them that love God, to them who are the called according to His purpose, for whom He did foreknow, He also did predestinate to be conformed to the image of His Son, that He might be the firstborn among many brethren. Moreover whom He did predestinate, them He also called; and whom He called, them He also justified: and whom He justified: them He also glorified (Rom. 8:29-30).

Hope Thou in God

For I know the thoughts that I think toward you, saith the LORD, thoughts of peace, and not of evil, to give you an expected end (Jer. 29:11).

One day while reading an article concerning the psychological affects that kids and adults face who are stricken with attention deficit disorder (ADD) and attention deficit hyperactive disorder (ADHD), I thought to myself, "surely this is an infirmity from the devil, the god of this world, who comes against God's handiwork." But, later on, I learned that the attacks from the devil may be introduced by allergies and deficiencies; perhaps brought on by the many different and improper foods we eat, and so on.

When my son was five years of age and in kindergarten, he was diagnosed with attention deficit hyperactive disorder (ADHD). Whenever I received the news of this report from a psychologist, I cried. Whether or not it was minor or major, it was overwhelming for me to think that he should have to suffer through such an ordeal. Later, I held myself accountable for perhaps not meeting all the nutritional requirements before, during and after pregnancy.

But, while in the midst of despair, the Lord spoke clearly to my spirit and said, "Why are you downcast? Surely your son is fearfully and wonderfully made for My service." From that point on I made a decision to be at peace, trusting in God to make up for all that is lacking in my son for now and throughout his life time. Praise God!

Point of Contact

We must educate ourselves concerning those things that concern us. Also, it helps to seek medical advice and attention from a good physician, then trust the great Physician. Now speak life to those dead things.

Longevity

Thou shalt come to thy grave in a full age, like as a shock of corn cometh in his season (Job 5:26).

They shall still bring forth fruit in old age; they shall be fat and flourishing; to show that the Lord is upright; He is my rock, and there is no unrighteousness in Him (Ps. 92:14-15).

My son, forget not my law, but let thine heart keep my commandments: For length of days, and long life, and peace, shall they add to thee (Prov. 3:1-2).

Hear, O my Son, and receive my sayings; and the years of thy life shall be many (Prov. 4:10).

Honour thy father and thy mother, as the LORD thy God hath commanded thee; that thy days may be prolonged, and that it may go well with thee, in the land which the LORD thy God giveth thee (Deut. 5:16).

The fear of the Lord prolongeth days: but the years of the wicked shall be shortened (Prov. 10:27).

With Long Life

How would you like to live a long life on this earth? Well, God has made a promise to us, His children concerning length of years:

With long life will I satisfy him, and show him My salvation. Surely life in itself is a mystery, and who can ever understand the mysteries of death? We simply must trust in God and accept that which is inevitable (Ps. 91:16).

We can also trust in God for considerable time on this earth. You know, God has also promised us seventy years and some may even live to be eighty (Ps. 90:10). Therefore, if we follow God's instructions and take care of our temple (our body), we may surely walk in this blessing.

In the book of 2 Kings, we understand that Hezekiah was at the point of death due to a dreadful illness he caught. But, he cried out to God in deep anguish and not long after, God delivered him from the power of death, adding fifteen years to his life (2 Kin. 20:1-6).

There's a mystery found in Scripture you know! It is written, "In a moment, in the twinkling of an eye, at the last trumpet: for the trumpet shall sound, and the dead shall be raised incorruptible and we shall be changed (1 Cor. 15:51-52).

Point of Contact

There isn't a magic potion for long life! Kings before us would testify to this, but there is a formula available to receive the unattainable from God. It's called prayer; let your heart's cry be known to Him.

SECTION II

Chapter Nine

Debt

*R*ender to Caesar the things that are Caesar's, and to God the things that are God's (Mk. 12:17).

For which of you intending to build a tower, sitteth not down first, and counteth the cost, whether he have sufficient to finish it? (Lk. 14:28).

If therefore ye have not been faithful in the unrighteous mammon, who will commit to your trust the true riches? (Lk. 16:11).

And it shall come to pass in that day, that his burden shall be taken away from off thy shoulder, and his yoke from off thy neck, and the yoke shall be destroyed because of the anointing (Is. 10:27).

Call unto Me, and I will answer thee, and shew thee great and mighty things, which thou knowest not (Jer. 33:3).

Owe No Man

Owe no man anything, but to love one another: for he that loveth another hath fulfilled the law (Rom. 13:8).

There are some wonderfully anointed books written concerning the freedom from debt. Books that offer insight and understanding about the way God wants us to operate with our finances. Many, in fact, inform us that being in bondage to debt is a curse from the devil. Why the devil? Because his chief purpose is to steal, kill and destroy (Jn. 10:10).

You see, the devil knows that if we have our finances in order, it will free us up to enjoy living life abundantly and that we will be able to carry out our spiritual duties where the Kingdom of God is concerned here on this earth.

Now that we know about the Devil's wicked attack against our finances, why are so many of us, even as Christians, still under attack? Really, I do believe that God wants us to be free from the devil's grip from such bondage. It is written, "I have come that they might have life, and that they might have it more abundantly" (Jn. 10:10). For me that means freedom from the awful bondage to the spirit of debt.

Years ago, the Lord shared His thoughts with me concerning the reason why the spirit of debt was still controlling my finances and causing me sleepless nights. I was in debt up to my neck in credit card bills, with bill collectors calling me everyday. Although I was a tither, God did not perform any major miracles for me until I sought Him in prayer to find out how I could help myself. He showed me that I was walking in disobedience where my finances were concerned: I was not a very good steward of my finances. The Lord brought to my understanding laws that govern His blessings, and I hindered my blessing because of disobedience.

I thought about this for some time and realized that I was not at all in line with God's will for the approval of financial prosperity. On the contrary, I could hardly stand to hold on to any money, not in a bank account, and definitely not in my wallet.

I discovered I needed a guide; something or someone who I was familiar with, or at least someone that handled money the way it should be handled: responsibly. Therefore, my mother came to mind with this divine management. She would say, "God will test you with those little things that you think you can't live without, and if you prove yourself worthy with little, He will put you in charge of a double portion."

I thank God that He is so merciful, because I'm still working on that process.

Point of Contact

Write out a plan for coming out of debt, commit yourself to it without sacrificing the necessary things, and devise a workable plan. However, keep in mind that consistency plus diligence plus prayer will further the progress.

Prosperity

Blessed is the man that walketh not in the counsel of the ungodly, nor standeth in the way of sinners, not sitteth in the seat of the scornful. But his delight is in the law of the Lord; and in His law doth he meditate day and night. And he shall be like a tree planted by the rivers of water, that bringeth forth his fruit in his season; his leaf also shall not wither; and whatsoever he doeth shall prosper (Ps. 1:1-3).

And God is able to make all grace abound toward you; that ye, always having all sufficiency in all things, may abound to every good work (2 Cor. 9:8).

But my God shall supply all your need according to His riches in glory by Christ Jesus (Phil. 4:19).

Beloved, I wish above all things that thou mayest prosper and be in health, even as thy soul prospereth (3 Jn. 1:2).

Silver and Gold

But seek ye first the kingdom of God, and His righteousness; and all these things shall be added unto you (Mt. 6:33).

I would like to think that God is overjoyed over the prosperity of His people. But now, what exactly is prosperity?

If you were to look up the word in the dictionary, you would probably find this definition: "The state or condition of being successful, especially financially." Well, according to the world's standards, that's about all it is. Back in the day – Jesus' day that is – it appears to most that Jesus lived in poverty. Some would suspect, however, that He was prosperous by way of hidden wealth – wealth that He often shared with the poor around Him. But, I believe that because He was steadfast in doing the will of the Father who sent Him, his needs were met accordingly through the gifts that were prevalent in Him.

One of my sisters shared a story with me concerning a first time author. She said that this person had written a book inspired by the Holy Spirit. Later, after her manuscript was completed, the Holy Spirit instructed her to send copies of the book to consumers free of charge. Well, as it turned out, through her obedience, this first time author was blessed with such a financial harvest that her barns were overflowing (if you know what I mean). I was amazed at hearing the outcome of it all, but I was not surprised. You see, God's desire is that His children prosper (3 Jn. 1:2).

But, wait a minute, there is an order to this kind of prosperity that includes seeking His kingdom and His way of operation. I believe that whenever we seek God's will concerning the gifts that He has instilled in us and use them wisely, being prayerful always, we may begin to understand that real prosperity is worth much more than silver and gold.

Point of Contact

If prosperity by way of wealth could buy me the world, but I had no love for self, or my fellow men, could I depend on prosperity through wealth to buy that too?

Giving

Honour the Lord with thy substance, and with the firstfruits of all thine increase: So shall thy barns be filled with plenty, and thy presses shall burst out with new wine (Prov. 3:9-10).

Will a man rob God? Yet ye have robbed Me. But ye say, Wherein have we robbed Thee? In tithes and offerings (Mal. 3:8).

And I will rebuke the devourer for your sakes, and he shall not destroy the fruits of your ground; neither shall your vine cast her fruit before the time in the field, saith the Lord of hosts (Mal. 3:11).

Give, and it shall be given unto you; good measure, pressed down, and shaken together, and running over, shall men give into your bosom. For with the same measure that ye mete withal it shall be measured to you again (Lk. 6:38).

And God is able to make all grace abound toward you; that ye, always having all sufficiency in all things, may abound to every good work (2 Cor. 9:8).

Seed Time, Harvest Time

Every man according as he purposeth in his heart, so let him give; not grudgingly, or of necessity: for God loveth a cheerful giver (2 Cor. 9:7).

One day an old friend of mine and I were on the phone chatting about this and that when the mailperson came around to drop off the mail; I interrupted our little conversation and went to get it. Upon doing so, I discovered a check in an envelope in my name. Really! I was not expecting any money. Not from a long lost aunt, forgotten uncle, or Mr. Magoo for that matter, but there it was. I ran to the phone to tell my friend of my small fortune. She paused for a short time, and then said, "Oh my goodness, I can't believe it! But, then again, you're a tither – you love to give."

Now the next thing she said had me laughing so much, I could hardly contain myself. She said, "That's it! I'm gonna pick up every piece of jewelry I bought, pawn them, and pay my tithes as soon as possible."

Well, after letting her go to do whatever she thought best I went about my own day. But, after awhile of thinking about the leftovers we as God's children hand over to him, I felt more inclined to cry rather than laugh.

Back in the day when I was a carnal thinker, I'd ask myself time and time again, "Now what in the world does God want with my money, and why is tithing such a big deal anyway? Why is it that every time you look at a preacher, you see a dollar sign printed on his forehead with a smile and a handshake? Besides, aren't gifts freebies from God?"

"My goodness, why in creation do I have to take my almost invisible earnings and give it to some preacher? I mean after all, God isn't going to come down from heaven to collect the money and buy bread for those in need. On the contrary, how do I know that the needy are getting my money anyway?"

Would you believe, all of that grumbling over two dollars and fifty cents?! As if my measure of inadequacy could actually pierce a hole through the pits of hell; maybe it could, perhaps yours might! Especially if the two dollars and fifty cents was all you had to offer, and like the woman in the Bible who gave from her need, not her excess, and with a cheerful heart. I'm sure then indeed the Lord would open the windows of heaven and pour out multiple blessings that we would not have room (peace, joy, healing, wisdom, understanding, favor) enough to receive it.

Point of Contact

"Payment due after services are rendered!" This is the message that you may find in most doctor's offices, and we don't seem to have a problem with it. "He wants his money!" Therefore, let us renew our mind according to God's directive concerning our giving to Him, what actually belongs to Him, so we might be blessed.

Success

This book of the law shall not depart out of thy mouth; but thou shalt meditate therein day and night, that thou mayest observe to do according to all that is written therein: for then thou shalt make thy way prosperous, and then thou shalt have good success (Josh. 1:8).

Trust in the Lord with all thine heart; and lean not unto thine own understand (Prov. 3:5).

In all thy ways acknowledge Him, and He shall direct thy paths (Prov. 3:6).

The steps of a good man are ordered by the Lord: and He delighteth in his way (Ps. 37:23).

Eye hath not seen, nor ear heard, neither have entered into the heart of man, the things which God hath prepared for them that love Him (1 Cor. 2:9).

That the blessing of Abraham might come on the Gentiles through Jesus Christ; that we might receive the promise of the Spirit through faith (Gal. 3:14).

Blessed be the God and Father of our Lord Jesus Christ, who hath blessed us with all spiritual blessings in heavenly places in Christ (Eph. 1:3).

Whose Ya Daddy?

The Spirit of the Lord is upon Me, because He hath anointed Me to preach the gospel to the poor; He hath sent Me to heal the brokenhearted, to preach deliverance to the captives, and recovering of sight to the blind, to set at liberty them that are bruised, to preach the acceptable year of the Lord (Lk. 4:18-19).

Travel back with me in time if you will, to a place, a city – the synagogue where Jesus made His mark of success. Listen as the story unfolds: A group of self-righteous, overly religious folks sat quite still with their heads lowered, as to worship, when suddenly a tall, stately young man, commonly dressed, walked up to the podium. After humbling Himself before the Holy Scriptures, He announced deliverance through Him, then He concluded: "This day is this scripture fulfilled in your ears" (Lk. 4:21).

"Say what?" yelled one of the leaders from the corner of the room.

"What the..." said another.

"Who in the world does this man think He is?"

"Say man, looka here! Who died and made you king?"

"Yea!" said one other person: "As If!"

Still another: "Say man, awh! Who's ya' daddy?"

"One of the leaders from the synagogue spoke saying, His daddy is Joseph, you know: The old carpenter who lives down the road over yonder, around the back alley."

Finally, one of the men walked over to Jesus and said, "Look man, I'll tell ya' what. Why don't ya' find some wood, a few scrapes of metal, a decent hammer, and go open shop someplace? Yea! That's what you need, but, awh... leave the ministering to us guys, alright?"

Jesus smiled encouragingly, realizing that the question before Him: "Who's ya' daddy," spoken by these seemingly wise, successful men, was an actual invitation for the Spirit of God to show up and show out in the life of Christ.

No, there were no accolades to Jesus' account. No one danced a jig, and there were no standing ovations, but the Spirit of His "Daddy" performed mightily through Him, throughout His public ministry.

Point of Contact

When God opens a door, no man can shut it. When He closes a door, no one can open it. Therefore, do not be too concerned about who you know or don't know; consider the fact that God is the only one who can move mountains. Ask Him to bless your efforts and if that isn't enough, ask Him to bless you with divine favor.

Chapter Ten

Miracles

*T*hou shalt also decree a thing, and it shall be established unto thee: and the light shall shine upon thy ways (Job 22:28).

With men this is impossible; but with God all things are possible (Mt. 19:26).

For verily I say unto you, that whosoever shall say unto this mountain, Be thou removed, and be thou cast into the sea; and shall not doubt in his heart, but shall believe that those things which he saith shall come to pass; he shall have whatsoever he saith (Mk. 11:23).

And God wrought special miracles by the hands of Paul: So that from his body were brought unto the sick handkerchiefs or aprons, and the diseases departed from them, and the evil spirits went out of them (Acts 19:11-12).

He therefore that ministereth to you the Spirit, and worketh miracles among you, doeth he it by the works of the law, or by the hearing of faith? (Gal. 3:5).

The Greatest Miracle

But as many as received Him, to them gave He power to become the sons of God, even to them that believe on His Name: Which were born not of blood, nor of the will of the flesh, nor of the will of man, but of God (Jn. 1:12-13).

Nowadays, folks scoff at the thought of a miracle and others fail to recognize it even when it's staring them in the face. Perhaps this is because we do not understand the love of God.

After the death and burial of my mother, my own strength and healing of that accident happened almost immediately – my body with all of its pain was healed miraculously. But even more miraculous was my transformation. My old self as it was with its ugliness died alongside my mother in that car. Although I didn't understand what was taking place, the Holy Spirit had began a work in me right then.

Like the miracle that Jesus performed in Cana during a wedding by turning water into wine, like so, whenever we are broken, a miraculous transformation begins. For some, the fear of denouncing a past lifestyle may prolong this transformation, but He who has begun a good work in you will perform it until the day of Jesus Christ (Phil. 1:6).

The testimony of a transformed life is surely the greatest miracle ever told.

Point of Contact

If a miracle is what you need, be steadfast in prayer and know that God is still in the miracle working business. Keep in mind that sometimes the answer to your miracle may be right in your midst.

Saints

Gather My saints together unto Me; those that have made a covenant with Me by sacrifice (Ps. 50:5).

But the saints of the most High shall take the kingdom, and posses the kingdom even forever and ever (Dan 7:18).

There is therefore now no condemnation to them which are in Christ Jesus, who walk not after the flesh, but after the Spirit (Rom. 8:1).

Grace be unto you, and peace, from God our Father and the Lord Jesus Christ (Col. 1:2).

Giving thanks unto the Father which hath made us meet to be partakers of the inheritance of the saints in light: Who hath delivered us from the power of darkness, and hath translated us into the kingdom of His dear Son: In whom we have redemption through His blood, even the forgiveness of sin (Col. 1:12-14).

This Is How We Do It

For whom He did foreknow, He also did predestinate to be conformed to the image of His Son, that He might be the firstborn among many brethren. Moreover, whom He did predestinate, them He also called: and whom He called, them He also justified: and whom He justified, He also glorified (Rom. 8:29-30).

C'mon, say it with me: "We fall down, but we get up, we fall down, but we get up; for a saint in just a sinner who fell down, but couldn't stay there, and got up."

Are you a Christian? You know, born again, spirit-filled, washed in the blood. If so, thank God for your redemption through His Son, Jesus.

Now, are you walking in sin? I mean struggling with some secret sin, being caught up in the moment, perhaps backsliding? Well, do you know that there's good news for you as a child of the King: "Just get up again!" Sounds impossible? Well, with man, it is impossible, but with God, nothing is ever impossible... nothing at all.

One day an old colleague of mine stopped by my home to visit, then sat down, and the two of us began chatting about this and that when, before long, she began making unkind remarks about those who call themselves Christians but walked in sin. She appeared to be deeply frustrated, perhaps because she was battling some secret sin and looking for a way of escape. But there I sat quite still and gave her my undivided attention as though in a stupor, but really trying to understand what she saw that angered her so in those who were under the blood, but not without faults and weaknesses.

I said, "Well, to me a Christian is someone who is able to identify sin in self as well as others, but then walk in a spirit of compassion and forgiveness towards their fellow man."

"You see," I continued, "the world at large throws stones for stones; you know, an eye for an eye. But a genuine Christian, though imperfect, and still struggling with weaknesses and battling the world, the flesh, and the devil, looks on another Christian brother and sees what God does: a blood washed soul."

Point of Contact

Don't sweat the small stuff! As imperfect beings, we're bound to fall down, but Jesus paid the price for us that we might get back up again and be down with foolishness and sin. Therefore, let's bear with one another.

Salvation

Verily, verily, I say unto thee, except a man be born again, he cannot see the kingdom of God (Jn. 3:3).

For God so loved the world, that He gave His only begotten Son, that whosoever believeth in Him should not perish, but have everlasting life (Jn. 3:16).

That if thou shalt confess with thy mouth the Lord Jesus, and shalt believe in thine heart that God hath raised Him from the dead, thou shalt be saved (Rom. 10:9).

Giving thanks unto the Father, which hath made us meet to be partakers of the inheritance of the saints in light: Who hath

*delivered us from the power of darkness, and hath translated us into
the kingdom of His dear Son: In whom we have redemption through
His blood, even the forgiveness of sins (Col. 1:13-14).*

*And it shall come to pass that whosoever shall call on the Name of
the Lord shall be saved (Acts 2:21).*

Cold Turkey

The spirit is indeed willing, but the flesh is weak (Mt. 26:41).

Lynn's grandmother had been praying for her for what seemed like ages,
but Lynn didn't know it. Whenever they spoke to one another – mainly this
happened when Lynn needed money to pay her rent – at the close of the short
conversation, her grandmother old Ida would say, "Wade not long in the valley
of decision, chile."

Not long after the last conversation between Lynn and her grandmother,
old Ida passed on and the remaining family was called in for the reading of the
will. Whenever Lynn's name was called to receive what her grandmother had
left her, she discovered five crisped one hundred dollar bills, the amount she
always borrowed to pay her rent, and with it, a stationary with the words,
"Wade not long in the valley of decision, chile."

That night, Lynn could not sleep, and the next day, she refused to eat.
Little by little she grew tired of running from whomever, or whatever it was
pulling at her heartstrings, but she didn't know her way through the process.

Because of the faithfulness of her grandmother's prayers, Lynn had come
to a fork in the road, a collision course with God. You see, it wasn't that God
needed to call her grandmother home for Lynn to even consider having a little
talk with Jesus. It was the fact that old Ida's work on earth was done – no
doubt God had bigger fish for Ida to fry.

While on earth, her prayers for her grandchild had swung open the throne
room doors of heaven and the aroma of old Ida's praise was like a sweet
smelling scent in the nostrils of God. The decision to accept Him was sorely in
the hands of Lynn.

Lynn couldn't help but realize that something was up, but she quickly decided that it wasn't worth losing any sleep over. Besides, the girl was worldly and therefore not willing to give in without a fight. Huh! You mean she should give up her romance with the world to surrender to a man she'd never met and had very little knowledge of? What, are you kidding?

Nevertheless, the pull at her heartstrings continued, but this time it was much stronger. Why, some nights she'd make her bed on the floor of her little closet, shutting the door behind her, hoping that perhaps this feeling would go away or at least be made difficult to rest on the heart of a person who could barely stand up in that cramped up little space, much less sleep in it. She was right, because God is a gentleman; He patiently stands at the door knocking.

Weeks turned into months, when finally, the girl could take it no more; she fell on her knees, hoping to cut a deal with God. "Okay, Lord," she said, "I promise that from now on I'll be in church every Sunday. But, oh, by the way, I don't do Wednesdays. See, I know how much these church folks love their study... besides, I don't even own a Bible; so you see I wouldn't know my way around it. Shoot, until recently, I thought Genesis was, ah, that dude Adam's old lady."

"Now God, since we're having this conversation, I might as well get it all out. You see, I like to party! Ah, like twice a week, but since I'm getting older, I'll slow it down for ya' a bit. Oh, and Lord, there's somethin' else. Please don't be angry when I tell ya', but I likes my 'stuff' if you know what I mean. Not to mention my 'boo,' Roy; of course, you probably know him by Leroy. That's Daddy! I love me some, Daddy."

"Whew! That felt good. Lord, I really enjoyed talking to ya', and now that we've had this conversation, I believe everything's gonna be alright."

One month later, during a Sunday service that usually lasted for about two and a half hours, the service lasted a bit longer for Lynn. On that particular Sunday, Lynn met the man whom she had never really known. The Spirit revealed him to her through a song sung by a little old lady who looked very much like old Ida, her grandmother. Why, even Lynn gasped when she saw her.

The little old lady sang, "Wade in the water," and though her voice trembled, she sang with such depth and such conviction until Lynn began crying, almost uncontrollably. Before the little soloist reached the third verse of the song, Lynn fell on her knees, crying out to God, then asking the Lord Jesus to make room for Himself in her heart.

That afternoon, Lynn returned to her place, a brand new person, refusing to look back.

"Behold! I make all things new" – Jesus (Rev. 21:5).

Pray this prayer: Lord Jesus forgive me, Lord Jesus receive me. I accept you now as my Lord and Savior: Thank you.

Point of Contact

No joke, lingering in the valley of decision will eventually pull you all the way down.

———

Hell

For great is thy mercy toward me: and thou hast delivered my soul form the lowest hell (Ps. 86:13).

But the children of the kingdom shall be cast out into outer darkness: there shall be weeping and gnashing of teeth (Mt. 8:12).

Then shall He say also unto them on the left hand, Depart from Me, ye cursed, into everlasting fire, prepared for the devil and His angels (Mt. 25:41).

For the wrath of God is revealed from heaven against all ungodliness and unrighteousness of men, who hold the truth in unrighteousness (Rom. 1:18).

Even as Sodom and Gomorrha, and the cities about them in like manner, giving themselves over to fornication and going after strange flesh, are set forth for an example, suffering the vengeance of eternal fire (Jude 1:7).

Jaws Uncensored

And whosoever was not found written in the book of life was cast into the lake of fire (Rev. 20:15).

"Well now, what's a nice person like you, doing in a place like this?"

Whatever your worst nightmare, your most embarrassing moment, the most appalling pain that ever engrossed your physical body, your most horrible fears, or even the hottest summer of your life on this planet: Just forget it... forget all of it, because hell is a whole lot worse.

Do you know that some people actually think that hell is a figment of an old demented soul's imagination?

Yea right, as if life as we know it, is the end of this story.

Point of Contact

I could give you several good reasons for not wanting to go to hell, but let's try this one: The words "It's getting hot in here" will never be understood.

Chapter Eleven

Bondage

*H**ear my cry, O God; attend unto my prayer from the end of the earth will I cry unto Thee, when my heart is overwhelmed: lead me to the rock that is higher than I (Ps. 61:1-2).*

And I will walk at liberty: for I seek thy precepts (Ps. 119:45).

Now the Lord is that Spirit: and where the Spirit of the Lord is, there is liberty (2 Cor. 3:17).

Stand fast therefore in the liberty wherewith Christ hath made us free, and be not entangled again with the yoke of bondage (Gal. 5:1).

But whoso looketh into the perfect law of liberty, and continueth therein, he being not a forgetful hearer, but a doer of the work, this man shall be blessed in his deed (Jas. 1:25).

Live, My Brother

There is the way which seemeth right unto a man, but the end thereof are the ways of death (Prov. 14:12).

Whenever someone mentions the word "prison," most people think of a large secluded area with a huge building, secured with bars and guards. The truth is, many of us are in prison in our own minds through compromise, ungodly traditions or perhaps, as one well-known preacher would say: "stinkin' thinkin'."

One day, a friend told me a story about a young man who was in prison; a man whom the Lord wanted to set free from the chains that bound him with a supernatural breakthrough. One night, an angelic being visited him, disguised through rays of light. As he stared curiously at the being, the chains and shackles that were on his wrists and ankles fell to the floor and the door to his cell opened wide. Instantly, the young man started toward the cell door without a word, then suddenly, he remembered his secret sins, those unrestrained desires, and by hook or by crook his determination to succeed. With this in mind, he then backed away from the cell door, and there he remains, in prison.

Strangely enough, many of us are facing the same dilemma as this young man. Although, not in a padded cell, we remain in prison in our mind with Satan as the gatekeeper. In our fight to conquer the world, we struggle with bitterness, deception, and other mind games. But my prayer for you today is that you would be renewed in the spirit of your mind.

Point of Contact

Documenting untold fears, desires, and despondent thoughts is a step towards freedom; now seek those who can speak godly words of wisdom.

Fear

Thou shall not be afraid for the terror by night; nor for the arrow that flieth by day; Nor for the pestilence that walketh in darkness; nor for the destruction that wasteth at noon day (Ps. 91:5-6).

No weapon that is formed against thee shall prosper; and every tongue that shall rise against thee in judgment thou shalt condemn. This is the heritage of the servants of the Lord, and their righteousness is of Me, saith the Lord (Is. 54:17).

Casting down imaginations, and every high thing that exalteth itself against the knowledge of God, and bringing into captivity every thought to the obedience of Christ (2 Cor. 10:5).

There is no fear in love; but perfect love casteth out fear: because fear hath torment (1Jn. 4:18).

Haunting Spirits

For God hath not given us the spirit of fear; but of power, and of love, and of a sound mind (2 Tim. 1:7).

When I was a child, I assume fear derived from normal tendencies, like it was natural to be afraid of strange sounds coming from an old house after everyone had gone to bed and the house settled, or the unusual squeaking from old hardwood floors causing you to feel like someone was walking behind you. Yet, whenever I was afraid of anything, my mother would say, "Just call on the Name of Jesus, he'll take care of whatever's frightening you." Well, I did, and sure enough, the Lord did comfort me that I might rest in His love and get some sleep. No doubt, he knew that, having a sound mind, even though, sleep is what was needed in order to cast down imaginations. But, as time proceeded, those things I understood as normal tendencies felt more like unwelcome visitors.

Indeed, there are different types of fear. There's a holy fear of God where wisdom begins; there is an emotional fear, which is a fear of the unknown; and then there is fear that is tormenting, and not of God, nor does it derive from natural tendencies. This type of fear is most unusual and is of the adversary, the evil one. Still, not even the devil is capable of performing his bewitchery without some help, an invitation perhaps; like folks being religiously involved in the craft: witchcraft.

When I was a girl, I learned of the goings-on concerning witchcraft from the happenings around me. You see, this kind of lifestyle seemed to be a favorite pastime for the folks who knew the trade. My own grandfather who (praise God) surrendered his life to the Lord before going home to be with Him, was one of the tradesmen, and although he was not the kind of person easily moved even by one more compelling than he, sometimes conversing with the enemy is all that's needed for deception to begin. Well, with my own kinfolks dabbling with things they knew very little of, it was easy for the adversary, to initiate spirits to torment us with fear.

My dad was innocent concerning such things, knowing very little about "voodoo" as we carelessly put it, or anything else in the spirit world; needless to say he was a needless target where the devil was concerned. My mom, on the other hand operated in direct opposition to the enemy's bewitchery, walking after Godly precepts, and meeting all of the necessary requirements to tear down the enemy's strongholds. Nevertheless, because of the seed that was sown throughout the years, this opened the door to generational curses and a spirit of fear; but thanks be to God, I am redeemed.

Point of Contact

If you knew there was a thief in your neighborhood, would you leave your doors unlocked? I would hope not. Therefore, consider this piece of information: welcoming ungodly devices, no matter what they are, is like asking a wrong spirit into your home to conduct all of it's affairs, and eventually bring about destruction.

The Past

For Thou art my hope, O Lord God: Thou art my trust from my youth (Ps. 71:5).

And thine ears shall hear a word behind thee, saying, 'This is the way, walk ye in it, when ye turn to the right hand, and when ye turn to the left' (Is. 30:21).

Behold, the former things are come to pass, and new things do I declare: before they spring forth I tell you of them (Is. 42:9).

Remember ye not the former things, neither consider the things of old. Behold, I will do a new thing; now it shall spring forth; shall ye not know it? I will even make a way in the wilderness; and rivers in the desert (Is. 43:18-19).

Therefore we are buried with Him by baptism into death: that like as Christ was raised up from the dead by the glory of the Father, even so we also should walk in newness of life (Rom. 6:4).

I am crucified with Christ: nevertheless I live; yet not I, but Christ liveth in me; and the life which I now live in the flesh I live by the faith of the Son of God, who loved me, and gave Himself for me (Gal. 2:20).

Apron Strings

Brethren, I count not myself to have apprehended: but this one thing I do, forgetting those things which are behind, and reaching forth unto those things which are before, I press toward the mark for the prize of the high calling of God in Christ Jesus (Phil. 3:13-14).

Have you ever tried walking into your future while stumbling over those things from your past? I mean, even memories of the way things use to be when life was simple. Many of us do from time to time, and some of have never stopped; without realizing it, we simply refuse to be delivered from those things that are behind us.

A certain family member had been incarcerated for a short length of time, due to an addiction. There is something I recently learned and it is this: the devil isn't always our worst enemy. The majority of the time, we are our own worst enemy. Therefore, I think it is safe to say that not every addiction is about the possession of demons, but our lower self-nature that invites us to seek out those things that coincides with the enemy's plans for us.

Once he returned home, he was blessed with provisions that enabled him to begin again, and though he appeared to be content, there was something distant about him. Any amount of time in confinement might captivate the thoughts and cause the emotions to become alarmed; and to add to the difficulty, the world, the flesh, and the devil will work hand in hand to remind you of past failures and shortcomings in order to keep you in bondage for the certainty of your destruction.

While visiting with him, I sensed a void that no words could fill. He looked discouraged, as if doomed to failure. Worse yet, his anchor was nowhere to be found, to catch him before he went down again. Oh, he tried to play it off, walking around with a strut, but whenever he thought no one was looking, the inner man surfaced, and again there was a look of discouragement. How do you reach out to someone so close, yet so far?

It did appear that the memories of "what used to be" had become something on which to base his hopes, even with those things that prevented him from pressing into his future with hope. I would imagine to him life was simple back then with all of its difficult battles. No doubt, he was able to make it through with little or no effort, but then why not? Life is simple when you're hiding behind apron strings.

I felt sorry about his discouragement and hoped that in some small way I might make a difference in his life. Perhaps I could help to loosen the chains of the past. Therefore, I tried explaining to him the importance of surrendering one's life to Christ, but then I was reminded by other family members of our need to operate in the natural realm, you know, to handle things logically. I agree, but are we not, all of us, three-fold beings? Do we not live in a physical body, and have a soul, and a spirit, the very thing that connects us to God. Look, the body is dying because of sin. So what do you do when you are drowning? On whom do you call when your life is being snuffed from under you? Tell me! Is the Creator of all humanity really that foreign to us?

Perhaps the speed with which time passes will help to heal those old wounds of the past... perhaps. But, just in case it doesn't, the Lord stands at the door of our heart, knocking and waiting to tear down those walls of the past, and set our foot on a firm foundation.

Point of Contact

True, the familiarities of the past can be helpful in pointing us in a better direction, but never wanting to leave will only cause us to take three steps forward and two steps back continuously. Developing a system, perhaps documenting where you are in life at the moment, and where you would like to see yourself in time to come, will usher you towards a better tomorrow.

Chapter Twelve

Rest

M y presence shall go with thee, and I will give thee rest (Ex. 33:14).

For thus saith the Lord God, the Holy One of Israel; in returning and rest shall ye be saved; in quietness and confidence shall be your strength: and ye would not (Is. 30:15).

Thus saith the Lord, stand ye in the ways, and see, and ask for the old paths, where is the good way, and walk therein, and ye shall find rest for your souls (Jer. 6:16).

Come unto Me, all ye that labour and are heavy laden, and I will give your rest. Take My yoke upon you, and learn of Me; for I am meek and lowly in heart: and ye shall find rest unto your souls. For My yoke is easy, and My burden is light (Mat. 11:28-30).

Again, he limited a certain day, saying in David, to day, after so long a time; as it is said, To Day if ye will hear His voice, harden not your hearts (Heb. 4:7).

I Miss My Time With You

Martha, Martha, thou art careful and troubled about many things: but one thing is needful; and Mary hath chosen that good part, which shall not be taken away from her (Lk. 10:41-42).

"I miss my time with you, those moments together; but you're busy... busy trying to serve me, take care of the family and earn a little money– I understand! Except who will fill you when you are empty? Once you have served me, cared for your family, and earned a little money."

During a season, the Lord advised me to pull back from what I later recognized as one enormously stressful workload. I had been ripping and running almost non-stop, working up a sweat. What's worse is I had little or no interest in that particular field of study. If I might add, the need to stand out compels the adrenaline to put on a show and with it, a desire to continue in the struggle. But on this particular day, after huffing and puffing, just trying to get from one place to the next on time, He clearly impressed these words upon my heart: "Daughter, simplify your life."

I quickly spoke up, "How Lord? I'm already caught up in the shuffle; there's just so much to do, and accomplishments do not happen without some kind of responsibility you know.

"Besides, the rush is almost necessary. It's difficult out here just to get a parking spot – it's a mad house here." I continued talking to the Lord while dodging cars. "I'm ashamed, Lord, You know, I really don't give much time to prayer anymore. You see, it takes all the strength I have to get up minutes earlier even to get to class on time, and besides, I see my son for only thirty minutes a day, and I talk to Him for about fifteen. I'm really sorry," I said.

For the moment, the Lord left me to my forlorn state of affairs, but then whenever I sat still long enough, I heard Him say to me, "You will never find satisfaction in doing what I have not designed you to do, but you will find fulfillment in doing what I have called you to do." I stood there looking hopelessly entangled, as though caught in a web. However, after evaluating the situation at hand, I willingly surrendered my over bearing schedule before the Lord and asked Him for the courage and strength to walk in obedience.

Point of Contact

With this ever-changing world we live in, sometimes it is difficult to take some time out and get in touch with our inner self in time alone with God. However, it is vital that we take some time out, to not only refresh our bodies and minds, but our spirits as well.

Anointing

Then Samuel took the horn of oil, and anointed him in the midst of his brethren: and the Spirit of the Lord came upon David from that day forward (1 Sa. 16:13).

Behold, O God our shield, and look upon the face of thine anointed (Ps. 84:9).

And it shall come to pass in that day, that his burden shall be taken away from off thy shoulder, and his yoke from off thy neck, and the yoke shall be destroyed because of the anointing (Is. 10:27).

The Spirit of the Lord is upon me, because He hath anointed Me to preach the gospel to the poor; He hath sent Me to heal the brokenhearted, to preach deliverance to the captives, and recovering of sight to the blind, to set at liberty them that are bruised, To preach the acceptable year of the Lord (Lk. 4:18-19).

Superman

But the anointing which ye have received of Him abideth in you, and ye need not that any man teach you: but as the same anointing teacheth you of all things, and is truth, and is no lie, and even as it hath taught you, ye shall abide in Him (1 Jn. 2:27).

What is the anointing? Tell me, what exactly does it feel like to be anointed anyway? Surely most people would like to know. In fact, I used to ask myself these questions even though I could never really comprehend the magnitude of its power.

What? Did I hear you say that the anointing is the burden removing, yoke destroying power of God? Well, what in the world is that, and how might I get it?

The woman I knew as mother did not know the anointing by name, though it was operative in her life. I know this now because things which were relatively impossible for her to accomplish, through her efforts alone were made feasible through the power of God's Spirit.

What, you mean you've never heard of Superman? The man with x-ray vision, the person who could leap tall buildings in a single bound. Hypothetically speaking, Clark Kent, better known as Superman, was an ordinary man made of flesh and blood. However, when he stepped into that phone booth, a transformation took place. A supernatural power surged through his entire being, enabling him to do the impossible. Sounds superficial? Well, it doesn't for those who understand the Spirit who raised Christ from the dead. On the contrary, that same Spirit wants to quicken our mortal bodies that we might do great exploits.

One evening while looking outdoors through my patio window, I looked upward towards the sky. I have always enjoyed looking up there simply because God uses it as a canvas to paint some of the nicest visual displays and perhaps messages, if you're looking close enough. During this time, I witnessed something rather unusual. It was made known to me by way of clouds. Looking up, I saw what appeared to be a large paintbrush that immediately took on the shape of the flame of fire that is described in the book of Acts (2:3), which descended over the heads of those present at the time of Pentecost.

I stared at it curiously, wondering if a revelation might follow. Then a long stem reached out to a row of little figures that resembled men, causing each figure to grow larger, though without losing shape. With this, the cloud that was shaped like a large paintbrush began to disappear, however, retaining its shape. I was amazed and excited at the same time. Indeed, the anointing is the burden-removing, yoke-destroying power of God, and whenever it is present, it empowers man's ability increasing his capacity for the glory of God.

Point of Contact

Because God's Spirit dwells on the inside of me, I'm anointed! I can do all things through Christ Spirit.

Intercession

And He was numbered with the transgressors; and He bare the sin of many, and made intercession for the transgressors (Is. 53:12).

For the law of the Spirit of life in Christ Jesus hath made me free from the law of sin and death (Rom. 8:2).

Who is he that condemneth? It is Christ that died, yea rather, that is risen again, who is even at the right hand of God, who also maketh intercession (Rom. 8:34).

Confess your faults one to another, and pray one for another, that ye may be healed. The effectual fervent prayer of a righteous man availeth much (Jas. 5:16).

Prodigal Son II

It was meet that we should make merry, and be glad: for this thy brother was dead, and is alive again; and was lost, and is found (Lk. 15:32).

One day while visiting my family, I saw one of my brothers at my uncle's house down the street. I had not seen him during my previous visits back home so I was glad to see him standing there. At once, I jumped out of my car that was parked over at my sister's home and with a hand in the air, I waved to him. The instant I got his attention, he immediately walked over and visited with me. But then, as I looked up at him, I noticed him staring at me, and the look on his face appeared to be a cry for help. Still I went about my day, even my visit there feeling carefree.

Upon returning to my home, the Holy Spirit brought my brother to mind and I could not help but remember the look on his face, as if to say, "I'm in shackles, Syl, bound by old habits that I can't seem to shake off, so let's just say our goodbyes, and I'll be on my way." Immediately following, I made a decision to intercede for him, to stand in the gap until he is free to serve the Living God as his spirit longs for him to do.

You know, those who cannot find their way may not verbally wish to share this news with us. However, the Spirit of God can help us discern their waywardness. Intercession is far different from saying, "Lord, remember my family members. Amen." It is pleading to God for the needs of those who may be unable to plead for themselves. It is standing in the gap in prayer, tearing down the enemy's stronghold over the lives of those who grip our heartstring.

It's calling those things that be not as though they were; looking to Jesus, the Author and finisher of our faith.

Point of Contact

Interceding for others may very well open the door to the manifestation of our prayer request: Keep the faith.

Prayer

Praying always with all prayer and supplication in the Spirit, and watching there unto with all perseverance and supplication for all saints (Eph. 6:18).

Be careful for nothing; but in every thing by prayer and supplication with thanksgiving let your requests be made known unto God. And the peace of God, which passeth all understanding, shall keep your hearts and minds through Christ Jesus (Phil. 4:6-7).

Confess your faults one to another, and pray one for another, that ye may be healed. The effectual fervent prayer of a righteous man availeth much (Jas. 5:16).

Nail on the Head

If ye abide in Me, and My words abide in you, ye shall ask what ye will, and it shall be done unto you (Jn. 15:7).

Whenever a prayer request of ours seemingly went unanswered, my mother would say to us, "Perhaps, you did not hit the nail on the head." Hitting the nail on the head meant praying with wisdom, that is, asking the Holy Spirit for spiritual wisdom that we might know exactly what the root of the problem was and present it to God that the prayer request might be answered. Like Bartimaeus did when Jesus ask the question, "What wilt thou that I should do unto thee?" Bartimaeus did not ask for a hundred dollars, or even friends, he simply said, "Lord, that I might receive my sight" (Mk. 10:51).

Missing the nail on the head in prayer means another round of prayer concerning the same matter. It is not that God forgets, or simply denies the request; it is just that He is more concerned with the root of a matter more than the surface of it.

My mother was a prayer warrior! I recognized this about her even when I was a child. Thus, prayer was never something obscure to me. In addition to her entreaty to God through prayer, she was able to make poignant steps to the throne room for the pressing needs of others. There was no need of x-ray vision, or mystical goggles to understand that she knew her way around the throne room. From her point of view, time in prayer meant visitations from God, and visitations meant answered prayer and an understanding of God's ways.

During a season, not long ago, I began praying about a particular desire that appeared important to me. While in fellowship with the Lord, the Spirit of God said to me, "The problem is, you are not hitting the nail on the head; remember that God is wanting to take care of the root of this matter, more than the surface of it." I thought about it for a moment and remembered how my mother always seemed to know exactly what to pray about, always hitting the nail on the head. But then again, her decision to abide in God's word made it possible for spiritual visitations, and spiritual visitations predetermines answered prayer.

Point of Contact

God's delays are not necessarily God's denials; they very well may be for those who choose to spend little or no time in prayer. Simple, short prayers are better than no prayer at all.

Witnessing

How beautiful upon the mountains are the feet of him that bringeth good tidings, that publisheth peace; that bringeth good tidings of good, that publisheth salvation; that saith unto Zion, Thy God reigneth! (Is 5:2-7).

Go ye therefore, and teach all nations, baptizing them in the name of the Father, and the Son, and of the Holy

Ghost (Mt 28:19).

But ye shall receive power, after that the Holy Ghost is come upon: and ye shall be witnesses unto me both in

Jerusalem, and in all Judaea, and in Samaria, and unto the uttermost part of the earth (Acts 1:8).

Silent Witness

...And it shall turn to you for a testimony (Lk. 21:13).

How do you become a witness to others about this abundant life that Jesus is waiting to share with them?

Perhaps by standing on a street corner, proclaiming the way to salvation, or possibly by handing out bibles on a bus, spreading the word concerning the saving knowledge of our Lord Jesus. No doubt many have been converted to

Christ through those means. And why not? Perhaps there wasn't anything jamming the flow to which the Spirit could move about. But, what about those who refuse to come to Christ because they prefer to remain in the valley of indecision?

A year ago, I had a talk with the Lord concerning an unsaved co-worker; who happened to be weighed down with a series of trials and afflictions. While in fellowship with Him, I asked, "Lord how can I make you known to this person who I work so closely with everyday? It's quite clear that she needs your help. The things that she speaks of seem to be a job for you and you alone. I would like to be of some help to her, but I do not wish to chase her away." You see, she was callous, rigid, and distant, with a look that clearly stated, "Don't even think about it! I've heard it all before." Therefore, with this kind of feedback, I managed to hold my peace.

However, after a short while, just through casual conversation, I learned that her entire family was saved. "But I'm the only devil!" she bluntly stated. No problem I thought; after all, God has one too and he knows exactly what to do with him. Just then, even as I was about to share with her the favor of the Lord for those who are made partakers of Christ inheritance through his redemptive blood, the inner witness impressed upon my heart to silently minister to her. "How do I do this," I wondered. After praying this, He responded, "By becoming a walking testimony. 'I have planted, Apollos watered; but God gave the increase'" (1 Cor. 3:6).

Point of Contact

Asking God's help to creatively influence others is a plus. However, a pleasant attitude is an additional benefit.

God's Will

I will bless the Lord, who hath given me counsel: my reins also instruct me in the night seasons (Ps. 16:8).

Shew me thy ways, Lord, teach me thy paths (Ps. 25:4).

Lead me in thy truth, and teach me: for thou art the God of my salvation; on thee do I wait all the day (Ps. 25:5).

For this God is our God for ever and ever: he will be our guide even unto death (Ps. 48:14).

Trust in the Lord with all thine heart; and lean not unto thine own understanding (Prov. 3:3).

If any of you lack wisdom, let him ask of God, that giveth to all men liberally, and upraided not; and it shall be given him (Jas. 1:5).

It is Well With My Soul

Father, if thou be willing, remove this cup from me: nevertheless not my will, but thine, be done (Lk. 22:42).

Whenever we are facing a dilemma and our back is against the wall, we have the opportunity to go through the fire with our eyes focused on Him, and be at peace; even in the midst of the storm, or fall out and complain; wondering, "why me?" When Jesus was in the garden of Gethsemane, he humbly surrendered his will to the Father that he might gain a surpassing victory, defeating the works of the devil; even death.

How can we know and understand the will of God in any circumstance? How can we determine if our will coincides with his?

When my son was about five years of age, he began complaining of what appeared to be excruciating headaches. As a result, I took him to see his pediatrician, hoping to learn of the problem, but no answers were found; nothing specific anyway. Therefore, I manage to control his distress with a child's pain reliever and the laying on of hands, asking God for his healing mercy to heal those broken places in my son's body. Like any parent in this predicament, I almost wished that I could carry his distress on my shoulder, even if only for a little while. The thought of receiving a bad report concerning my son was one of those things I was not prepared to deal with. But do you know that in order for God to prove his might in any circumstance, your faith must rest on His love. The fact that he loves us enough to handle not just uncomfortable reports but whatever needs to be dealt with in between.

As time progressed, one evening, my son walked into the room where I was and said something to me that caused my knees to give way beneath me. He said, "Mommy, Jesus is calling me!" I tried to make some earthly sense of what he meant, so I said, "Oh no Ben, remember the story that I read to you about Samuel?" (1 Sam. 3:4-10). "Well," I continued, "God is probably trying to get your attention in some small way." He looked up at me puzzled, as though he could not believe that I had suddenly taken leave of my senses. So he carefully said, "Okay mommy, but I'm telling you."

Suddenly, I turned my head to the window, and stared at what was left of the day, while drops of warm tears stream down my face. My eyes focused on a cloud of smog on my window, and for some reason I found comfort in it as though the Lord could be found there. Then I simply said "He's my only son, you know, please don't take him from me." I think in all my years of talking to God, this was the most solemn request I have ever made.

Let me just say, like any Christian parent, I've always prayed with my son and even read Bible stories to him, making sure he understood the importance of keeping God in your daily life. But, the thought of mentioning things like heaven or anything related to paradise was never something I found to be of much importance, especially for a child of this age; I simply could not think of a reason to make mention things of that nature. But, my son stood before me and described heaven: even the Father, the Son, and the Holy Spirit there, in such a way that in my mind made even the biblical description of it in the book of Revelations seem vague.

The only words that came to mind are words spoken by my dad as he lay on that hospital bed, realizing that this time in his life cancer had won. "It's just one of those things" he said, and I will never...never forget those words. That's what I felt, and when I could no longer stand the agony of it all, I fell on my knees that Sunday morning and cried out, "Lord, I understand! Your will be done." Then, as if I knew He were waiting to here something else, I said, "I'm gonna love you anyway, you know that you're my life." At that moment, I felt heaven and earth stand still, and I could see the Lord sighing a sigh or relief with His healing power.

A couple of weeks later, my son was scheduled for a CAT scan by a specialist and his diagnosis confirmed that a small cyst was found on his sinus cavity. I praise God because when Jesus surrendered His will, the stripes he bore brought about healing for all.

Point of Contact

Having an understanding of God's love may help us understand that all things somehow work together for the good of them who love God and are called according to his purpose (Rom. 8:28).

Chapter Thirteen

Gratitude

*O*ne generation shall praise Thy works to another, and shall declare Thy mighty acts (Ps. 145:4).

I will speak of the glorious honour of Thy majesty, and of Thy wondrous works. And men shall speak of the might of Thy terrible acts: and I will declare Thy greatness (Ps. 145:5-6).

Take, eat; this is My body. Drink ye all of it; For this is My blood of the new testament, which is shed for many for the remission of sins (Mt. 26:26-28).

Neither do I condemn thee: go, and sin no more (Jn. 8:11).

Let the Word of Christ dwell in you richly in all wisdom; teaching and admonishing one another in psalms and hymns and spiritual songs, singing with grace in your hearts to the Lord (Col. 3:16).

By Him therefore let us offer the sacrifice of praise to God continually, that is, the fruit of our lips giving thanks to His Name (Heb. 13:15).

Sharing Mary's Joy

Then took Mary a pound of ointment of spikenard, very costly, and anointed the feet of Jesus, and wiped His feet with her hair: and the house was filled with the odour of the ointment (Jn. 12:3).

One day, while I was in a small cafe in Memphis, Tennessee, just vacationing with my husband and son, I noticed a Christian program on television at the bar. There were several people seated at that bar and though some of them might have been a little intoxicated, each one watched with intense interest to the man who shared his testimony of the goodness of God.

Then at once, another person, who perhaps was feeling convicted over some sin in her life, made a quick gesture to the waitress who was standing nearby, signaling her to change the channel. Naturally, she stole the attention of those whose eyes were fixed on the man who was sharing his testimony, and this seemed to please her more than anything. Then, as if this were not enough, she then uttered a few words as if to mock uncommon things, further disrupting the movement that was taking place right there in that little cafe.

Quickly then without any warning, she, for whatever reason, caught my eye, and while she stared, she sneered at me. I remember looking back at her and felt sad for those like her who look but cannot see. Suddenly, I began to think of Mary's gratitude to Jesus for His awesomeness. One of the reason's I love to praise my heavenly Father is because I am so grateful to Him. I am grateful because He has chosen me, I'm grateful for His loving arms. I'm just so grateful.

I'll never forget the moment, the very second, my brother told me my mom died. There I lay in the hospital with severe internal injuries. My doctor had suggested to my family that the news of my mother's death not reach my ears, therefore my uncle and my brother walked into my room with cold bewildered faces. Looking up at them, I ask, "How is she?" As though I were honestly expecting them to say, "Oh, she's fine, a few cuts and bruises, but she'll be alright."

Instead, my uncle looked down at me without saying a word. Perhaps he thought it best to respect my doctor's medical advice, not wanting to cause me any further physical harm and still remain true to himself by telling me something that wasn't so. But, my brother, with his head positioned down, and a tone in his voice as if commissioned by God for this seemingly small task said, "She died, Syl!" For a quick second, I felt completely disoriented.

Then, I felt like screaming from the top of my voice; hoping the emptiness that overwhelmed me would vanish into thin air; instead I felt as though I were out on a ledge, and I was falling. Just then, the comforting arms of my wonderful Savior held me at that very moment and spoke peace to the storm that would have swept me away.

No, I will never forget those words from my brother announcing my mother's departure, nor will I forget the tone in his voice when he spoke them.

But then – this one thing I know and will never forget – the loving arms of comfort from the Savior held me at that very moment, and continued to hold me even through those midnight hours and, yes, through the years that followed.

For this, I have to say to those who mock the things of God: "Please don't mock me for sharing Mary's joy over such a wonderful Savior, because you weren't there when he put His loving arms around me, and you don't know the cost for this, my gratitude."

Point of Contact

A grateful heart is a giving heart! Whenever we're grateful to someone we wish to express our gratitude.

Praise

I will praise Thee, O Lord with my whole heart; I will show forth all Thy marvelous works (Ps. 9:1).

Rejoice in the Lord, O ye righteous: for praise is comely for the upright (Ps. 33:1).

Praise the Lord with harp: sing unto Him with the psaltery and an instrument of ten strings. Sing unto Him a new song; play skillfully with a loud noise (Ps. 33:2-3).

I will bless the Lord at all times: His praise shall continually be in my mouth (Ps. 34:1).

O magnify the Lord with me, and let us exalt His Name together (Ps. 34:5).

Enter into His gates with thanksgiving, and into His courts with praise: be thankful unto Him, and bless His Name (Ps. 100:4).

Just Because

Bless the Lord, O my soul: and all that is within me, bless His holy Name (Ps. 103:1).

What is praise? Well all I can say is, "When I think about how much the Lord's given me, without limitations, and no series of worn out religious rules, I'm filled with wonder at how His love has touched my life. Therefore, this devotion that I practice is a welcome sacrifice. From what I see, this kind of worship was primed distinctly for me. A kind of praise I never knew was here in me: So, I praise Him..."

"Just because...He is awesome.
Just because...He is all that.
Just because...He is mighty.
Just because...He is holy.
Just because...He is the Savior.
Just because...He is the healer.
Just because...He is trustworthy.
Just because...He is victorious.
Just because...He is Righteous.
Just because...He is more than enough.
Just because...He knows the end from the beginning.
Just because...His hand rules the world.
Just because...He has already defeated the devil.
Just because...He cannot lie.
I praise Him just because."

Point of Contact

Begin by praising God for a brand new day. Praise Him because you woke up in your right mind. Praise Him because your limps are still strong, and your family still loves you. Praise Him simply because you're still here.

Praise Him because you're not laying in some gutter with no place to go and no one to turn to. And, if you are, then praise Him because His mercy is new every morning, and you still have a chance to pull yourself up by the collar.

Praise Him for the simple meal on your table, and the fact that you still have work to do. Now do you still feel like complaining? Let us praise the Lord!

Thanksgiving

Let us come before His presence with thanksgiving, and make a joyful noise unto Him with psalms (Ps. 95:2).

Enter into His gates with thanksgiving, and into His courts with praise: be thankful unto Him, and bless His Name (Ps. 100:4).

For all things are for your sakes, that the abundant grace might through the thanksgiving of many redound to the glory of God (2 Cor. 4:15).

Giving thanks always for all things unto God and the Father in the Name of our Lord Jesus Christ- (Eph. 5:20).

Blessing in Disguise

That I may publish with the voice of thanksgiving, and tell of all Thy wondrous works (Ps. 26:7).

It seems rather difficult, if not impossible, to give thanks to God when seemingly there's nothing to be thankful for. However, the Bible says, in every thing give thanks: for this is the will of God in Christ Jesus concerning you (1 Th. 5:18).

Some years ago, before the thanksgiving holiday, my family faced a major crisis in the area of finances... there weren't any. Although my parents were hard working folks and my mother was a wise shopper, there comes a time when faith must be tested.

Now only a few precious days away before sitting down to thank God for all the many blessings we received throughout the year, mother realized that certain bills demanded attention. Therefore with the little money saved up for a thanksgiving feast, even that belonged to the creditors.

Now at this time, not only was our pantry empty, but the thought of even a simple meal was unheard of, at least from the way things looked in a natural sense. At that point, mother got alone with God and began thanking Him for what she knew He was able to do, and because He is the God of more than enough, she knew He would provide.

Most assuredly He did, through the most obvious resources available: blessed hands, and seven children. Together, we manage to do odd little jobs, thus making provisions for the best thanksgiving feast ever.

Our Father knows what things we need, even before we ask Him; therefore, let us give thanks.

Point of Contact

In all you're getting, get understanding! (Prov. 4:7) Contrary to popular belief, prosperity (God's idea of it, anyway) is much more than just money. It is also peace of mind, health to your body, and joy unspeakable. Don't hesitate to thank God for the small stuff.

Chapter Fourteen

Grace

*B*e glad ye children of Zion, and rejoice in the LORD your God: for He hath given you the former rain moderately, and He will cause to come down for you the rain, the former rain, and the latter rain in the month (Joel 2:23).

Moreover the law entered, that the offence might abound. But where sin abounded, grace did much more abound (Rom. 5:20).

But by grace the grace of God I am what I am: and His grace which was bestowed upon me was not in vain; but I laboured more abundantly than they all: yet not I, but the grace of God which was with me (1 Cor. 15:10).

Wherefore gird up the loins of your mind, be sober and hope to the end for the grace that is to be brought unto you at the revelation of Jesus Christ (1 Pet 1:13).

Needful Things

My grace is sufficient for thee: for my strength is made perfect in weakness (2 Cor. 12:19).

There's a way to love those who appear to be unlovable through God's anointing. Although this may take a little faith, lots of prayer, and wisdom on our part, God's grace is a sustaining power that enables us to stand even in the midst of hard times and poor choices. On the contrary, for many of us, God's grace is the only thing that keeps us going.

As little girls my sisters and I enjoyed playing with dolls, pretending to be real mommies, while the daddies, though imaginary, were like knights in shining armor. You see, as little girls it was easy to think of a male figure as a husband, the knight in armor. After all, your imagination will always allow you to make believe. Except in reality, what happens when your knight turns out to be a nightmare, and eventually your hopes and dreams of a relationship in marriage become shattered?

There are many things responsible for a split-up in a marriage. Division is a distinct problem that, sadly, can tear that relationship apart. Things said, or perhaps left unsaid that left a deep wound to a fragile heart.

One day, I asked the Lord to bless me with a happy, well-balanced marriage. Surely, it is God's will that His children are happy, especially in marriage. Therefore, I knew that I was praying according to His will for my life and marriage.

Let me just say that I have always admired mature-thinking couples; those who are knowledgeable concerning what is right and good in the midst of chaos and differences, ungodly influences and charm. So, I strongly desired this for my own marriage and decided to lay this prayer request at the Lord's feet. But immediately after my time alone with Him, His Spirit impressed these words on my heart "My gracious favor is all you need; my power works best in your weakness.'' He continued, "Some times the very thing you consider imperfect and uncomfortable are the things that draw you closer to me." I thank God for His grace, the sustaining power that enables me to stand.

Point of Contact

Some things are really too difficult for us to handle on our own. True! There are many resources available to take care of our needs, but peace of mind is something this world can't give: something that is only present when we welcome the Spirit of Jehovah Shalom in midst of our circumstances.

———

Love

This is My commandment, that ye love one another, as I have loved you (Jn. 15:12).

Though I speak with the tongues of men and of angels, and have not charity, I am become a sounding brass, or a tinkling cymbal (1Cor. 13:1).

And though I have the gift of prophecy, and understand all mysteries and all knowledge; and though I have all faith, so that I could remove mountains, and have not charity, I am nothing (1 Cor. 13:2).

Charity suffereth long, and is kind, charity envieth not; charity vaunteth not itself, is not puffed up, doth not behave itself unseemly, seeketh not her own, is not easily provoked, thinketh no evil; rejoiceth not in iniquity, but rejoiceth in the truth; Beareth all things, believeth all things, hopeth all things, endureth all things (1 Cor. 13:4-7).

Charity never faileth (1Cor. 13:8).

No Greater Love

Greater love hath no man than this, that a man lay down his life for his friends (Jn. 15:13).

How do we begin to understand the love of God? How can we fathom the depth of this, His unconditional love? Does He really love me?

When I was growing up, I hardly knew my dad. Oh yes, he lived in the same house as I did, ate the same foods, and breathed the same air. Still, I did not truly know him. He was quiet and at times appeared to be a deep thinker, as though silently putting his thoughts together to be written to form a book. An easy-going man was he, one who enjoyed the simple pleasures in life, and respectfully speaking, one who enjoyed this world, and whom this world enjoyed.

Reared in a home where his dad's presence was void, I suppose it was sort of difficult for him to find his way around as a dad, and difficult enough to show any signs of love and affection.

"Albert, do you love me and the kids?" My mom would ask him as each new year rolled in. With something that sounded like words, he'd mumble a response that you couldn't make out if you tried. Oh men, they can be so macho. Even more so, the world, the flesh, and the devil can bear up heavily against the vitality of a man until about all the poor souls can do is mumble.

You know, the devil would actually bombard heaven, if he could, in order to destroy the courage of a man and rob him of what's rightfully his – to rob him of his reasons for living and, yes, his ability to love unconditionally and to be loved unconditionally.

"I'll die for my family!" Were the words of my dad to my mom as he lay there on that hospital bed; physically deteriorating, yet spiritually invigorated, as if God's Spirit of vitality had supercharged him to make known his reason for being on this earth for such a short time. Upon hearing these words, my mom never doubted my dad's love for her or his children ever again. That day, I learned of the dad I never knew. I learned of this his love for me, his child that went beyond words. That's what God's unconditional love for us identifies with; something beyond words: There is no greater love! Thank you, Jesus.

Point of Contact

Keep a mental picture of those who appear to be unlovable; then ask God to see them through His eyes. God sees what we see and what we do not see in others.

Mercy

But as for me, I will come into Thy house in the multitude of Thy mercy: and in Thy fear will I worship toward Thy holy temple (Ps. 5:7).

To the Lord our God belong mercies and forgiveness, though we have rebelled against Him (Dan 9:9).

Who is a God like unto Thee, that pardoneth iniquity, and passeth by the transgression of the remnant of His heritage? He retaineth not His anger forever, because of thee (Mic. 7:18).

And His mercy is on them that fear Him for generation to generation (Lk. 1:50).

And the grace of our Lord was exceeding abundant with faith and love, which is in Christ Jesus (1 Ti. 1:14).

His Mercy Endures

But God, who is rich in mercy, for His great love wherewith He loved us, even when we were dead in sins, hath quickened us together with Christ, (by grace ye are saved) (Eph. 2:4-5).

As a young adult, I was rebellious in a quiet sort of way. Good or bad, my thoughts and actions were my own, and with just a look, I would dare you from interfering with whatever it was I chose to do or think. Oh yes, I loved the Lord; in my opinion, He was to me, a knight in shining armor, and I was the apple of His eye... until He decided that enough was enough.

Several months before my mom went home to be with the Lord, she asked me to put pen to paper concerning my shortcomings, or sins, if you will. Though embarrassed to present myself on paper that way, I did what she asked and unloaded all of my filthy laundry, so to speak, out in the open. Upon reading my list of trespasses, she then lifted them up to God in prayer, as though standing in the gap for me, that my many grievances would be forgiven. Then after doing this, she said something that sounded so mysterious. She said, "Your hit will not be hard!"

That was it! I looked right into her eyes, but I did not ask her the meaning of that statement. I didn't know whether or not its meaning was symbolic or literal, but then perhaps I really didn't want to know.

Not long after this meeting, my mother was killed in an accident that both she and I were victims in. Not long after that, the Lord allowed me to remember and understand the meaning of her statement: Know of His great mercy, and live to talk about it. Did God sustain me because He loves me? Yes! Did He sustain me because He has great plans for me?

Yes, again! But even through my many trespasses, His mercy endured.

Point of Contact

To understand God's mercy is beyond our human capability, but to extend mercy towards others is within our ability. We should ask God to teach us mercy, that we may show others mercy.

Obedience

But if thou shalt indeed obey His voice, and do all that I speak; then I will be an enemy unto thine enemies, and an adversary unto thine adversaries (Ex. 23:22).

Thou shalt not bow down to their gods, nor serve them, nor do after their works: but thou shalt utterly overthrow them, and quite break down their images (Ex. 23:24).

And ye shall serve the Lord your God, and He shall bless thy bread, and thy water; and I will take sickness away from the midst of thee (Ex. 23:25).

There shall nothing cast their young, nor be barren, in thy land: the number of thy days I will fulfill (Ex. 23:26).

If ye be willing and obedient, ye shall eat the good of the land (Is. 1:19).

Wherefore gird up the loins of your mind, be sober, and hope to the end for the grace that is to be brought unto you at the revelation of Jesus Christ; as obedient children, not fashioning yourselves according to the former lusts in your ignorance (1 Pt. 1:13-14).

A Deaf Ear

The Lord made not this covenant with our fathers, but with us, even us, who are all of us here alive this day (Deut. 5:3).

Nowadays, the world is so blinded by the "express yourself" mentality, that anything that challenges the character of an individual, ruffles the features, so to speak. On the contrary, a response to the not very difficult to understand word "obedience" might very well sound something like this: "If I want your opinion, I'll ask for it."

Our plausible excuses for turning a deaf ear to God's commands have been made to rest on the weakened knees of worldly leaders, and they, possessing little if any Godly ruling, take the whole idea and put it in a sealed enveloped, then debate whether or not it is a matter for church or state. They then absentmindedly allow every unstable individual this thought to enter their own state of mind: "If it feels good, do it!" Still, some wonder why this world is in such a bad state.

Whenever God gives an individual a mandate to deliver a message, that person labors in anguish, like that of a woman trying to give birth but the baby in the womb in resisting. I would imagine that it was not an easy task for our brother Moses to wait on God that He might receive the commands of the Lord, which are just as prevalent today as they were those many, many years ago.

These, God's Ten Commandments were not only written as a guide for mankind, but as a mark of distinction for those who would choose to receive and obey them.

Point of Contact

Accepting authority from those around us may help us understand how to walk in obedience to God.

Chapter Fifteen

Despair

*T*he Lord is my strength and song, and He is become my salvation: He is my God, and I will prepare Him an habitation; my father's God, and I will exalt Him (Ex 15:2).

Why art thou cast down, O my soul? And why art thou disquieted within me? Hope in God: for I shall yet praise Him, who is the health of my countenance, and my God (Ps. 43:5).

Blessed be the Lord my strength, which teacheth my hands to war, and my fingers to fight: My goodness and my fortress; my high tower, and my deliverer; my shield, and He in whom I trust; who subdueth my people under me (Ps. 144:1-2).

Wounded Soldier

My God, my God, why hast Thou forsaken Me? Why art Thou so far from helping Me, and from the words of my roaring? (Ps. 22:1).

There she was alone with seven growing children, aging parents, and a brother who lived a distance away. She looked worn, as though life had thrown at her one hard ball too many. Some she was able to throw right back in the enemy's face without it harming those she loved, still others made her journey difficult like the cross of Christ, down the road to Calvary.

"Hang in there!" were the words of a cousin as he drove by with a hand raised, as if to salute her. She smiled, then stared in the distance as if she was wondering to herself, "Where will I get the strength for the rest of the journey ahead?" I watched her as though looking through a windowpane. But then again, it seemed as though I was always looking through a window pane; being shy as a child I hardly said a word, but I was always around watching, listening, and feeling.

There I stood, still trying to study the thoughts disclosed from her facial expression, hoping that those few words from our cousin would somehow let her know that this too shall pass. But, the sudden illness, then death of her aging father, the thoughts of her gone, but not forgotten husband, and the pull from her seven children was perhaps a bit too weighty.

That which made the beauty of the words, "growing older gracefully!" sound like, "there's no rest for the weary." It almost seemed as if God had left her to waddle in her sea of despair alone, without the slightest bit of hope. I realize that sometimes it does appear as though God isn't listening, but then, whenever I get alone with Him and worship Him as Jehovah Shammah, my God who will never leave or forsake me, He provides me with the strength I need for the journey ahead. He further prepares me with the wisdom to know how to handle difficult situations and the courage to stand.

You see, God had given my mother enough strength to complete her journey in this life, and when I reflect on her many victories, I have to say that He was there all the time.

Point of Contact

Be prayerful! God alone knows what the future holds and sometimes what it holds can be most difficult to endure. Don't wait for tragedy to strike before calling on the Name of the Lord to deliver and strengthen you. In the meantime, live a balanced life.

Determination

If ye do return unto the Lord with all your hearts, then put away the strange gods and Ashtaroth from among you, and prepare your hearts unto the Lord, and serve Him only: and He will deliver (1 Sa. 7:3).

Follow Me, and I will make you fishers of men (Mt. 4:19).

Whosoever therefore shall be ashamed of Me and of My words in this adulterous and sinful generation; of him also shall the Son of man be ashamed, when He cometh in the glory of His Father with the holy angels (Mk. 8:38).

For I determined not to know anything among you, save Jesus Christ, and Him crucified (1 Cor. 2:2).

David's Army

For the Lord God will help me; therefore shall I not be confounded: therefore have I set my face like a flint, and I know that I shall not be ashamed (Is. 50:7).

In these last days, I do believe God is calling forth many young people to fulfill His will on the earth. God said, that He would pour out His Spirit on all people (Joel 2:28). Today, many a young people are taking a stand for the kingdom of God with fearless determination just as David did against the giant Goliath.

One morning our son, who at the time was quite young, made plans to take a short trip with his dad. He has always enjoyed going away with his dad so he was, thus, quite excited. However, in a split second, he decided not to go; even after I tried to persuade him. Indeed, I was surprised at his unexpected change of mind, especially since he understood that no plans were made for an adventurous weekend. Nevertheless, I went along with his decision, though somewhat puzzled.

Later on in the day however, while in prayer, I made known this concern to the Lord and He soon brought to my understanding that God knows those whom He has chosen and when He chooses an individual, He began preparing them. This can happen even early on for their particular journey in life. I soon understood that there was no need to worry because my son's spirit was being encouraged by God's in preparation for His army. Not long afterwards, my thoughts centered on David in the book of 1 Samuel. David, a shepherd boy was minding his own business, tending sheep, when the Spirit of the Lord caused him to rise up against the giant who defied the armies of God (1 Sam. 17:36).

This boy, David, determinedly stood against Goliath in the Lord's Name and was victorious, not only that day but throughout his life.

Stirred by the Spirit of the Living God within, wonder no more, because you probably will. You see, the "It's your thing, do what you wanna do" mentality is sweeping the globe, and in our modern day society it does appear "all that glitters is gold." However, there is renewed strength, vitality, and all that God has to offer – and He has more than you can possibly imagine – waiting for you in your lifetime, and in the world to come.

Point of Contact

Dare to be different! Lift up a standard against those things that may not be beneficial to you in the final outcome.

Endurance

But he that shall endure unto the end, the same shall be saved (Mt. 24:13).

Thou therefore endure hardness, as a good soldier of Jesus Christ (2 Ti. 2:3).

And so, after he had patiently endured, he obtained the promise (Heb. 6:15).

If ye endure chastening, God dealeth with you as with sons; for what son is he whom the father chasteneth not? (Heb. 12:7).

Beloved, think it not strange concerning the fiery trial which is to try you, as though some strange thing happened unto you: But rejoice, inasmuch as ye are partakers of Christ's sufferings; that,

when His glory shall be revealed, ye may be glad also with
exceeding joy (1 Pt. 4:12-13).

Comfort Zone

Wherefore seeing we also are compassed about with so great a
cloud of witnesses, let us lay aside every weight, and the sin which
doth so easily beset us, and let us run with patience the race that is
set before us, looking unto Jesus the author and finisher of our
faith; who for the joy that was set before Him endured the cross
despising the shame, and is set down at the right hand of the throne
of God (Heb. 12:1-2).

"Okay, class, put everything away, including your study book. I am
handing you a test: answer what you know."

"What!" cried the students, with a look of exasperation on their faces.
"What test? No one told us anything about a test."

"Oh, but I did," the teacher said. "Perhaps you were not paying attention."

Most people would agree with the thought: facing any of life's difficulties
can be quite unbearable, especially if you were never prepared for it, or not
paying attention when the warning signs appeared. Surely, God Himself will
lay bare to us the laws of nature if we chance going against them. Yet, there
are times when He will not make known a test until the testing is completed.
We simply must learn how to hang on to the horns of the altar by prayer and
faith in Him.

I thoroughly enjoy reading the book of Job; it is such a passionate text.
Job was a man of complete integrity and (not to mention) wealth, which was
all taken back when he was suddenly thrown into the den of affliction.
Searching for some reason or rhyme as to how such misery could overtake one
who devoted himself to the ways of God, Job was sick at heart.

During a season, I drew a parallel between self and old brother Job. In my
mind, I had reached a pinnacle in my spiritual walk with God that convinced
me of thinking, "well, we had it like that." Therefore, I assume I was able to
endure just about anything. You see, together God and I had won quite a few

battles; tearing down many of the enemy's strongholds, not to mention, my old bad girl ways, and because of that, I was feeling kinda' good.

But, one day, perhaps while the Lord was bragging on my steadfast faith in Him, the Devil threw a few words His way saying: "Awh, yea! Like I said, skin for skin. Sure, she loves God! Huh, I mean, who wouldn't? Surely, she finds comfort in your promises to her; a covenant which makes her a soul heir to all that you posses."

He went on, "But now step aside for a while, and make her question your love for her, and I promise you, she'll curse you to your face."

My point is this: Job knew of God's might, he knew that the earth belonged to God, and no one else. He understood that God was able to do whatever He wanted and no one could stop Him, but there was this one thing he was not very familiar with: God's love. The one thing that enables me to endure some of life's most challenging pressures is the fact that God loves me. If I am ever tempted to forget that, may I find comfort in a gentle breeze, the smile of a child, a word from the wise, the hand of my Father.

Point of Contact

Find a quiet place, a place where you can invite the Spirit of God. Now begin to cast your cares on Him: where the Spirit of the Lord is there is liberty (2 Cor. 3:17). Now thank God for His grace that enables us to endure under pressure.

Chapter Sixteen

Patience

Rest in the Lord, wait patiently for Him: fret not thyself because of him who bringeth wicked devices to pass (Ps. 37:7).

I waited patiently for the Lord; and He inclined unto me, and heard my cry. He brought me up also out of an horrible pit, out of the miry clay, and set my foot upon a rock, and established my goings (Ps. 40:1-2).

Better is the end of a thing than the beginning thereof: and the patient in spirit is better than the proud in spirit (Eccl. 7:8).

But the fruit of the Spirit is love, joy, peace longsuffering, gentleness, goodness, faith, meekness, temperance: against such there is no law (Gal. 5:22-23).

For ye have need of patience, that, after ye have done the will of God, ye might receive the promise (Heb. 10:36).

Wherefore seeing we also are compassed about with so great a cloud of witnesses, let us lay aside every weight, and the sin which doth so easily beset us, and let us run with patience the race that is set before us, looking unto Jesus the author and finisher of our faith (Heb. 12:1-2).

Broken Dreams

But they that wait upon the Lord shall renew their strength; they shall mount up with wings as eagles; they shall run, and not be weary; and they shall walk, and not faint (Is. 40:31).

Do you know that being patient is a necessity that we as individuals must obtain in order to reap the benefit of a peaceful existence. Besides, I would imagine that God isn't about to put much stock in humanity's outrageous need for "this instant." Once upon a time, just hearing the word "wait" made me want to jump up and down and scream like a toddler. I would become so furious over the thought of what I planned, prayed or strived for if it did not happen at the time I circled on my calendar. I usually ended up in tears or some other emotional upheaval that was not worth the drama.

During this distressing transition from adolescence to adulthood, my mother thought it best to help make that transition a little easier. One day after shopping, she walked into the house, in my room and handed me a small bag; she smiled as though whatever was inside would transform me into a different person over night.

Upon opening the bag, my eyes focused on an ordinary wall hanging made of brown crinkled paper, and one blooming rose laying beside a broken vase. It was a poem written to me unknowingly. First, it described this individual's closeness to a loving Father, and the need to hand Him those things that are broken or messed up in life. The meticulous care and patience of God was clear to see by the author's well-rounded description concerning the development of those things that we bring to Him. But then, the nit-picking of this individual who, perhaps, wanted Him to realize that if by chance He's incapable of pulling it off, or putting it all together in time, made it almost impossible for God to get anything done. To conclude, once this individual, like so many of us, grew tired of wrestling with anticipation, they politely removed the delicate matter from God's gentle, yet strong hands saying, "I'm sorry, but you're just too slow."

Whenever I finished reading that poem, that day, I hurriedly threw it to the corner of my room, hoping that the words would vanish from my thoughts just as quick – but it was not so. Instead, those words are imprinted on my mind and used to send off a red flag whenever I want to run ahead of God's plan and purpose.

The all to common phrase, "let go, and let God" can be mind-boggling to the persons who were created to take the world by storm. However, once you have taken it by storm, will anxiety through power allow you to have peace of mind?

Point of Contact

With this ever-increasing shake and bake world we live in, it is difficult to find a corner and spend time in the presence of the Lord that He might lead and direct our path. Still, our need for independence should never interfere with our dependence on God: Let us be prayerful always concerning patience.

Protection

Yea, though I walk through the valley of the shadow of death, I will fear no evil: for Thou art with me; Thy rod and Thy staff, they comfort me (Ps. 23:4).

Surely He shall deliver thee from the snare of the fowler, and from the noisome pestilence (Ps. 91:3).

He shall cover thee with His feathers, and under His wings shalt thou trust: His truth shall be thy shield and buckler (Ps. 91:4).

What shall we then say to these things? If God be for us, who can be against us? (Rom. 8:31).

Shadows

Because thou hast made the Lord, which is my refuge, even the Most High, thy habitation; there shall no evil befall thee, neither shall any plague come nigh thy dwelling (Ps. 91:9-10).

One night while I was asleep, I dreamt that one of my brother's was being pinned down by several men who appeared much larger in stature than he. Although, he was blessed with natural physical strength, the overwhelming attack from his adversaries made his fight difficult to overcome. The entire scene in that dream caused me to tremble with fright. I then sat up in bed and quickly mumbled a prayer to God for His protection, hoping perhaps, that He would get the job done. Instead, the pull in my spirit to intercede for Him continued but much stronger.

That night, I learned that interceding for someone is far different from reciting a few prayers to God; laboring hard in prayer is more like it. My brother was in trouble, even if only in the spirit realm, which can be far worse than that of the natural realm; at least in the natural realm you can see whom you're up against, or rather whose up against you.

That very night, I wrestled with my flesh that I might turn from slumber. Then on the other hand, I wrestled with my spirit that I might find it. Just then, the Spirit of God who revives me, instructed me to lay hold of the ninety-first chapter of Psalms; that which I had memorized upon my mother's request some years ago. Even as I prayed "For He shall give His angels charge over thee, to keep thee in all thy ways" (Ps. 91:11), I envisioned myriads of angels freeing my brother from the snare of the fowler.

Point of Contact

Not superman, but God is more powerful than a locomotive. On the contrary, no amount of bodybuilding can protect us from the supernatural strength of unseen forces that may come against us. Therefore, trust yourself and your family to God. Pray for His hedge of protection around you and your family today.

Stress

Trust in the Lord with all thine heart; and lean not unto thine own understanding (Prov. 3:5).

In all thy ways acknowledge Him, and He shall direct thy paths (Prov. 3:6).

Commit thy works unto the Lord, and thy thoughts shall be established (Prov. 16:3).

Be careful for nothing; but in every thing by prayer and supplication with thanksgiving let your requests be made known unto God. And the peace of God, which passeth all understanding, shall deep you hearts and minds through Christ Jesus (Phil. 4:6-7).

Finally, brethren, whatsoever things are true, whatsoever things are honest, whatsoever things are just, whatsoever things are pure, whatsoever things are lovely, whatsoever things are of good report; if there be any virtue, and if there be any praise, think on these things (Phil. 4:8).

Strung Out

Casting all your care upon Him; for He careth for you (1 Pet. 5:7).

I think most people would agree with the thought: "Stress is a silent killer!" Why? Because you can feel the affect of it for months at a time and never really realize that it's slowly destroying you.

During a season, I worried over my health, my finances, my family, and everything that had anything to do with my life. For sure, I had unintentionally allowed my thoughts to drift away from God being in control of things and, therefore, all I had to do was spend time in His presence and cast my worried mind on Him. But my lack of time in prayer intensified my fears, forcing me to magnify my problem; as a result, I ended up turning a mole hill into a mountain. So there I was, stressed out over things I could do nothing about on my own anyway. But one day, I asked the Lord for His help and this is what He said: "Sylvia, it is time for you to send your cares on a vacation."

"Where?" I asked, assuming He was actually referring to a particular place. But, He simply said, "Try the Twenty-Third chapter of Psalms, and when you do, begin to meditate on every verse as though you had written it yourself through personal experience." Now whenever I feel weighed down by situations far too overwhelming for me to handle, even trivial things, I turn to this chapter in my bible and soak up the blessings of the Lord.

Point of Contact

I've discovered these simple pleasures as great stress-busters: brisk walks, relaxing music, gardening, sewing, crocheting, trips to a full service salon (instead of a do it yourselfer), a good book, soothing herbal baths and healthy comedies.

SECTION III

SECTION 3

Chapter Seventeen
End Times
Heaven
Restoration

Chapter Eighteen
Faith
Gifts
Self Esteem

Chapter Nineteen
Enemies
Forgiveness
Respect
Anger

Chapter Twenty
The Bible
Revelation Knowledge
Victory
Wisdom

Chapter Twenty-One
Abuse
Attitude
Loneliness
Sorrow

Chapter Twenty-Two
Foolishness
Lust
Sex
The Tongue
Addiction

Chapter Twenty-Three
Sin
Strife
Temptation
Guilt

Chapter Twenty-Four
Holiness
Women
Men

Chapter Seventeen

End Times

F or the vision is yet for an appointed time, but at the end it shall speak, and not lie: though it tarry, wait for it; because it will surely come, it will not tarry (Hab. 2:3).

And ye shall hear of wars and rumours of wars: see that ye be not troubled: for all these things must come to pass, but the end is not yet (Mt. 24:6).

And this gospel of the Kingdom shall be preached in all the world for a witness unto all nations; and then shall the end come (Mt. 24:14).

But, beloved, be not ignorant of this one thing, that one day is with the Lord as a thousand years, and a thousand years as one day (2 Pet. 3:8).

Like a Thief in the Night

But the day of the Lord will come as a thief in the night; in which the heavens shall pass away with a great noise, and the elements shall melt with fervent heat, the earth also and the works that are in shall be burned up (2 Pet. 3:10).

The King is coming, the King is coming, thank God Almighty, the King is coming!

When I was a little girl, I encountered a most unusual dream. I dreamt that the world had ended by a devastating fire throughout the earth. Before that time however, everyone had been informed of the coming of Christ, but somehow the time was never right. Suddenly, without further warning, everyone was in a state of panic, while cities were being consumed by fire. People from all walks of life began crying out to God, hoping He would deliver us from a fate worse than death. Just then Christ appeared, the world ended, and so did my dream.

That morning, I awoke trembling, and as a child, I could not understand the significance of such an astonishing dream, or why I dreamt it. Later on in life, however, the Holy Spirit allowed me to remember this dream and God's wonderful mercy, preparing His children for whatever may be ahead; even as stones are thrown.

During the absence of my parents through their death, my sisters, brothers, and myself gathered together in our parent's home to simply draw strength from one another, and well, bask in the warmth of a familiar love. This was our comfort zone, and how wonderful it was.

But, after a short time, things were not the same; each one of us began to change in our own way. Some clinging to a familiar faith, others... well, it was time to experience life; after all, what are we living for? But, in the search to find ourselves, we encountered many other things that would lead us down an unknown path. A path that would soon disrupt the peace and purity of our meetings and even cause division in our thought patterns.

But it was during this time that the Spirit of God began preparing us for the end of what was a great legacy. As a result, there would be no surprises, no reason to panic, and surely no need to fear.

No! Perhaps the goings-on concerning the mysteries of earthly changes are not the mark of the end of time, but perhaps it is a warning signifying the whirlwind before the end.

Do not let the coming of Christ catch you unaware.

Point of Contact

If you knew beyond the shadow of a doubt calamity were about to strike, would you sit there and ignore the warning signs? I would hope not! Therefore, let us make every effort to secure our salvation.

———

Heaven

For behold, I create new heavens and a new earth: and the former shall not be remembered, nor come into mind (Is. 65:17).

In My Father's house are many mansions; if it were not so, I would have told you. I go to prepare a place for you (Jn. 14:2).

Nevertheless we, according to His promise, look for new heavens and a new earth, wherein dwelleth righteousness (2 Pet. 3:13).

Emerald City

And the building of the wall of it was of jasper: and the city was pure gold, like unto clear glass. And the foundations of the wall of the city were garnished with all manner of precious stones. The first foundation was jasper, the second sapphire; the third, a chalcedony; the fourth, an emerald; The fifth, sardonyx; the sixth, sardius; the seventh, chrsolyte; the eighth, beryl; the ninth, a topaz; the tenth, a chrysoprasus; the eleventh, a jacinth; the twelfth, an amethyst (Rev. 21:19-20).

Remember the movie *The Wizard of Oz*? Whenever I watch a program, I try to focus on the depth of its meaning, and for me one of the most memorable scenes in that movie was the moment that Dorothy and her friends arrived in emerald city. The look on their faces was almost out of this world, and one could not help but feel as though this place, emerald city, was also out of this world.

Several months before my mother went home to be with the Lord, my brother, who was in the Marines and stationed in North Carolina, sent her a postcard with a very unusual message. Hypothetically speaking, he described a city – somewhere on this earth – where there were no guns, wars or violence, a place where everyone lived in peace and harmony with one another. A city that was too beautiful to describe in its entirety. A glorious splendor where night was as bright as day, and your burdens seem to vanish in the wind. He described the goings-on of this place in such detail, and with such passion that one would almost think that he was dreaming.

Whenever I read the message on that postcard, I could only conclude that this place my brother had described was shown to him in the spirit; a vision of a place in preparation of a homecoming. A place known as heaven – the Holy City, God's eternal throne, the City of Angels. A place where only the righteous will enter and where there is no sadness, no sickness, no struggle, no death.

Point of Contact

Imagine being on a tropical island, a paradise where all of your worries and cares seem to vanish in the wind. Now hold fast to that thought as you continue your journey on earth.

Restoration

And His raiment became shining, exceeding white as snow; so as no fuller on earth can white them (Mk. 9:3).

But if the Spirit of Him that raised up Jesus from the dead dwell in you, He that raised up Christ from the dead shall also quicken your mortal bodies by His Spirit that dwelleth in you (Rom. 8:11).

It is sown in dishonor; it is raised a spiritual body. There is a natural body, and there is a spiritual body (1 Cor. 15:43).

Who shall change our vile body, that it may be fashioned like unto His glorious body, according to the working whereby He is able even to subdue all things unto Himself (Phil. 3:21).

Divine Makeover

...For this corruptible must put on incorruption, and this mortal must put on immortality (1 Cor. 15:53).

Sometime after the death of my mom, a friend of my brother painted a portrait of her from a picture given to him, that it might be presented to our grandmother as a birthday gift. Upon seeing the portrait, I became a tad uneasy.

The portrait, though beautifully painted, did not display a true likeness of my mother's appearance, not from my remembrance. In the portrait, I looked for gray hairs with a little thinning around the temple, but it was flawless.

Then I looked for other physical characteristics that one encounters through time that appears with age; still the portrait was perfect in every way, and I was puzzled. Immediately the Lord impressed these words upon my heart, "You see, the portrait is a reflection of what is, not what was. In heaven, those things that were imperfect on earth are no more; what I look upon is a finished product. That's the reason this portrait was presented to you this way, that your eyes might look upon what was perishable, and know that it is now imperishable."

In a moment, in the twinkling of an eye, at the last trumpet: "for the trumpet shall sound, and the dead shall be raised incorruptible, and we shall be changed" (1 Cor. 15:52-53).

Point of Contact

Whenever I look at the moon at night, the light is so bright until I could not possibly imagine getting close to it without melting. Therefore, I would imagine this tent, we occupy: though beautiful in its setting and it shines brightly, it still yearns to shine all the brighter.

Chapter Eighteen

Faith

*I*f you have faith as a grain of mustard seed, ye shall say unto this mountain, Remove hence to yonder place; and it shall remove; and nothing shall be impossible unto you (Mt. 17:20).

So then, faith cometh by hearing, and hearing by the word of God (Rom. 10:17).

But without faith it is impossible to please Him: for he that cometh to God must believe that He is, and that He is a rewarder of them that diligently seek Him (Heb. 11:6).

Whom having not seen, ye love; in whom, though now ye see Him not, yet believing, ye rejoice with joy unspeakable and full of glory: Receiving the end of your faith, even the salvation of your souls (1 Pet. 1:8-9).

The Hem of His Garment

Even so faith, if it hath not works, is dead, being alone (Jas. 2:17).

Be it mustard seed faith, combat faith, mountain moving faith, or well, thoughtless faith, nothing moves the power of God's hand without corresponding action.

Not long ago, I suffered a series of afflictions due to hormone deficiencies. Although I did not understand what was going on with my body, I knew the Lord was aware of what was going on with me, and that He was in control. This was similar to the story of the woman with the issue of blood who suffered while seeing many physicians, but all were to no avail (Mk. 5:26). I too checked in and out of doctors' offices and emergency rooms, all to no avail. Soon fear began to take hold of my senses, tearing away what little faith I mustered up.

Let me just say that the process to unwavering faith isn't easy, even though the reward for believing is attained through the smallest possible measure – a mustard seed. Nonetheless, I would imagine the Hall of Fame of faith is filled with persons who stumbled repeatedly down the icy slopes of doubt. Surely the temptation to relax in its cold clammy den have crossed the mind of some of the great mountain movers of faith, and why not? After all, the reward for believing isn't given to the quickest, but to the one who can endure to the end and still believe.

While pretending to believe in a God, who I hoped at this time was still concerned with what was going on with me, I began to study what real faith means to God. One day, a familiar preacher of faith sent me a letter, inviting me to spread the gospel through seed faith. After reading the letter, I felt that this was an opportunity for a miracle break, though I had been a partaker of spreading the gospel in this way in the past, the harvest intended was sorely for self.

Nevertheless, through the Spirit's leading, I purposed in my heart to disregard myself and walk in obedience so God's plans might be manifested in the lives of others. Once the seed was planted, the Lord impressed these words on my heart: "Now you've touched the hem of my garment! Daughter, you are loose from your infirmity."

What is faith? Faith, my dear friends, is the substance of things hoped for, the evidence of things not seen, and corresponding action.

Point of Contact

Feed your faith and starve your doubts to death with the Word of God, patience and prayer.

Gifts

So that you come behind in no gift; waiting for the coming our Lord Jesus Christ: Who shall also confirm you unto the end, that ye may be blameless in the day of our Lord Jesus Christ (1Cor. 1:7-8).

But every man hath his proper gift of God, one after this manner, and another after that (1 Cor. 7:7).

And this they did, not as we hoped, but first gave their own selves to the Lord, and unto us by the will of God (2 Cor. 8:5).

Meditate upon these things; give thyself wholly to them; that thy profiting may appear to all (1 Ti. 4:15).

If any man speak, let him speak as the oracles of God; if any man minister, let him do it as of the ability which God giveth: that God in all things may be glorified through Jesus Christ, to whom be praise and dominion for ever and ever Amen (1 Pt. 4:11).

Divine Purpose

I have glorified Thee on the earth: I have finished the work which Thou gavest Me to do (Jn. 17:4).

God has handed out an abundance of precious gifts to His children. Surely, our Lord Jesus was His ultimate gift to mankind, and the Holy Spirit, who empowers us with many special abilities that we might fulfill our divine purpose.

You know, many persons have passed on from this life without having recognized their divine assignment, and therefore, many talents have gone to the grave without having been nurtured and fulfilled. Perhaps it was due to the fear of failure, or maybe, just maybe, a fear of success.

My mother was blessed with a series of special gifts, including good organization skills, as well as spiritual gifts; gifts she shared openly with others and blessed them with. As a result, one day she decided to write her own autobiography, so she could creatively express her thoughts and testimonies on paper. Unfortunately, procrastination and perhaps the fear of failure, or success, prevented her from going full speed ahead with her dream.

Strangely enough though, a few days before going home to be with the Lord, a very close friend of the family witnessed her saying, "That's it! My work is done." She closed her Bible, and the next day, she was gone. Although I didn't realize it then (none of us did), her purpose had been completed with the help of God, as shepherd over the lives of those she blessed. Perhaps it is His plan to continue this good work through the lives of those she touched.

Listen! You may never have to stand in the spotlight, or make a special guest appearance, and your lot in life may not be fame and fortune. But perhaps God is calling you to let your light shine, no matter how small, so the world might take note of it and glorify Him who calls you.

Point of Contact

Forget about the large picture! Spend a little time alone with yourself and discover those things that you're able to do considerably well and with passion. Now zoom in on those things, and ask God to direct your steps.

Self Esteem

So God created man in His own image, in the image of God created He him; male and female created He them (Gen. 1:27).

The Lord will perfect that which concerneth me: Thy mercy, O Lord, endureth forever: forsake not the works of Thine own hands (Ps. 138:8).

Thou wilt keep him in perfect peace, whose mind is stayed on Thee: because he trusted in Thee (Is. 26:3).

I will praise Thee; for I am fearfully and wonderfully made: marvelous are Thy works; and that my soul knoweth right well (Ps. 139:14).

How precious also are Thy thoughts unto me, O God! How great is the sum of them (Ps. 139:17).

And hath raised us up together, and made us sit together in heavenly places in Christ Jesus: That in the ages to come He might shew the exceeding riches of His grace in His kindness toward us through Christ Jesus (Eph. 2:6-7).

I AM

For Thou hast made [me] a little lower than the angels, and hast crowned [me] with glory and honour (Ps. 8:5).

"I know I'm not all that I can be; my imperfections always seem to catch up with me. But as long as I abide in you, I know that I will make it; step by step through this journey; Lord, please hear my prayers."

I fled to my little corner of the world whenever I sensed the Lord leading me into becoming a vessel for His kingdom in the area of literature. "O Lord! Me, I ask? I wouldn't know what to say besides, I'm still a bit shy therefore, I'll just sleep on it, and who knows?" Yet, His Word declares: "I can do all things through Christ who strengtheneth me" (Phil. 4:13).

No doubt, most of us will be tempted to question our ability to perform a divine task or fulfill a dream. We might even procrastinate, due to the fear of intimidation. Like Moses, we may even question God's confidence in us, reminding Him of our inability; for surely it was Moses, the man whose faith moved the hand of God to part the sea. And was it not Moses who stood on the mountain then handed down the laws of God, the Ten Commandments to generations? Indeed, it was this great mountain mover of faith who stood in the Lord's presence and said, "Who am I, that I should go unto Pharaoh and bring the Israelites out of Egypt?" (Ex 3:11).

Consider this: Moses met the necessary requirements in becoming the next Pharaoh, the Prince of Egypt, but he received no natural training in becoming God's deliverer for the children of Israel. I would imagine Moses was concerned with whether or not he was the man for the job. After all, he did have a type of speech impediment, an imperfection to his credit. "And Moses said unto the Lord, O my Lord, I am not eloquent, neither here to fore, nor since thou hast spoken unto thy servant: but I am slow of speech, and of a slow tongue" (Ex 4:10). But then, God told him, "I will be with thy mouth" (Ex 4:15).

Indeed, many have had to battle the demons of fear due to an obvious weakness. No doubt, many have even surrendered their hopes and dreams to unconstructive words, and disapproved expressions. Still, I would imagine to God, the sight of a person weighed down by the influence of low self-worth is like a seed in the ground, a probable foundation for a tree.

Point of Contact

Want to know how I download my capabilities: I simply go to the Word of God and remind myself that I can do all things through Christ. I can have what He says I can have; I can be all that He says I can be – I am.

Chapter Nineteen

Enemies

L *et God arise, let His enemies be scattered: let them also that hate Him flee before Him (Ps. 68:1).*

When a man's ways please the Lord, He maketh even his enemies to be at peace with him (Prov. 16:7).

Thy children shall make haste: thy destroyers and they that made thee waste shall go forth of thee (Is. 49:17).

But I say unto you, love your enemies, bless them that curse you, do good to them that hate you, and pray for them which despitefully use you, and persecute you; that ye may be children of your Father which is in heaven: for He maketh His sun to rise on the evil and on the good, and sendeth rain on the just and on the unjust (Mt. 5:44-45).

What shall we then say to these things? If God be for us, who can be against us? (Rom. 8:31).

Be not overcome of evil, but overcome evil with good (Rom. 12:21).

Foe

Be sober, be vigilant, because your adversary the devil, as a roaring lion, walketh about, seeking whom he may devour (1 Pet. 5:8).

So you've come to do the devil's bidding have you? Well, what's it going to be today? Slander, oppression, malicious behavior, or death; no doubt you're on a mission, I can see it in your eyes, and your tongue is curbed for destruction. Tell me, isn't he quite busy destroying the nations without your help, or could it be that the high price he pays for wickedness makes you want to fall at his feet? Look, before you decide to do His bidding and before you decide to make him your god, know this: "'No weapon that is formed against thee shall prosper; and every tongue that shall rise against thee in judgment thou shalt condemn. This is the heritage of the servants of the Lord, and their righteousness is of me,' saith the Lord" (Is. 54:17).

Point of Contact

Sometimes, some things are best left unsaid: especially if you know that it will only lead to confusion and strife. Don't argue with the devil.

Forgiveness

And forgive us our debts, as we forgive our debtors. And lead us not into temptation, but deliver us from evil (Mt. 12:13).

For if ye forgive men their trespasses, your heavenly Father will also forgive you: But if ye forgive not men their trespasses, neither will your Father forgive your trespasses (Mt. 6:14-15).

And when ye stand praying, forgive, if ye have ought against any: that your Father also which is in heaven may forgive you your trespasses (Mt. 11:25).

Judge not, and ye shall not be judge: condemn not, and ye shall not be condemned: forgive, and ye shall be forgiven (Lk. 6:37).

Letter of the Law

Then came Peter to Him, and said, Lord, how oft shall my brother sin against me, and I forgive him? until seven times? Jesus saith unto him, I say not unto thee until seven times: but, until seventy times seven (Mt. 18:21).

Wow! How many times is that exactly? I remember asking one of my junior high school teachers this question and was surprised even at her response. She said, "Really, we are not to keep an account of the wrongs done to us; that is what our Lord meant." I received no revelation of that at the time, but later on, I learned that having an unforgiving heart could hinder God's blessing simply for refusing to forgive one another.

One day, after silently entertaining thoughts over a wrong done to me, I became furious and wondered what I might say as to retaliate against this person. At that moment, I was so upset that I refused to allow the Spirit of God to instruct me and heal my brokenness. Therefore, before I knew it, I had not only taken a bite of the forbidden fruit of unforgiveness, I was indulging myself, drowning in a sea of bitterness and self-pity.

During this time, I felt isolated from my other self – the person who yearns to be one with the Creator. So there I was, standing alone, harboring unforgiveness and the unnecessary weight that comes along with it. Soon after this, my thoughts were shady, causing me to think unproductively, and in my opinion prevented me from moving on to the next level.

Nevertheless, I managed to convince myself that I was not liable for the wrong done to me and, therefore, there was only one way to handle an occurrence of this magnitude: either through manipulation, which meant witchcraft, or walking around for the rest of my days with a chip on my shoulder.

Yet, through the conviction of the Holy Spirit, and some good common sense, I realized that since man's days are like the grass – here today and gone tomorrow – harboring unforgiveness was not worth the drama that it takes to allow pride to have its way. Therefore, without hesitation and a willingness to see this thing through, I inquired of the Lord saying, "I don't know how to forgive this person, for the wrong they've done to me, but please teach me how to forgive and help me walk in that forgiveness to bury the hatchet."

Within seconds, I felt a load, a heavy weight lifting right off of my shoulder. No, I did not say that choosing to forgive would make you feel like you just won the Kentucky Derby, because that doesn't happen. On the contrary, each new day will present the temptation to relinquish one's decision and creep back into unforgiveness and retaliation; but then again, who wants to room with misery?

Point of Contact

Try not to rehearse past offenses. Rather, confront the offender and express your feelings as calmly as you possibly can and, if at all possible, never in the midst of an audience. Redirecting a discussion plays an important role in solving difficult matters, and an appropriate tone of voice works wonders.

Respect

Thou shalt not avenge, nor bear any grudge against the children of thy people, but thou shalt love thy neighbor as thyself: I am the LORD (Lev. 19:18).

Though the Lord be high, yet hath He respect unto the lowly: but the proud He knoweth afar off (Ps. 138:6).

Of a truth, I perceive that God is no respecter of persons: But in every nation he that feareth Him, and worketh righteousness, is accepted with Him (Acts 10:34-35).

Let everyone of us please his neighbour for his good to edification (Rom. 15:2).

Honor Thy Neighbor

Therefore, all things whatsoever ye would that men should do to you, do ye even so to them: for this is the law and the prophets (Mt. 7:12).

So who is my neighbor? Anyone standing next to you is your neighbor; anyone in your neighborhood, anyone in your family, anyone in this world.

Nowadays most people assume that anyone with a good attitude toward their fellow men is wimpish and rather naïve. We've become so hyped on our self to the point that if anyone so much as stared at us for a second longer than necessary, their on our hit list. We have a tendency to intimidate the weak, and imitate the strong, even if it means destroying our own character.

In some of the books in the New Testament, we learn that Jesus was not only compassionate towards people, but He respected them as well. To their opinions and differences, He did not shun without first giving them some form of respect, even if it were simply to allow them to voice their difference of opinion. It did appear as though their thoughts, ideas and feelings were of some concern to him.

Often, I feel moved by God's Spirit to do what Jesus did, and do to others what I would like them to do to me. Then there are times when I feel challenged in my spirit to do to others what Jesus would have me do towards them in spite of what they do not do to me. This I accomplish with God's help and by putting myself in my neighbor's place.

Point of Contact

Remember that those who you consider as nobody may very well be the apple of God's eye.

Anger

Cease from anger, and forsake wrath: fret not thyself in any wise to do evil (Ps 37:8).

A soft answer turneth away wrath: but grievous words stir up anger (Prov 15:1).

A gift in secret pacifieth anger: and a reward in the bosom strong wrath (Prov 21:14).

To give light to them that sit in darkness, and in the shadow of death, to guide our feet into the way of peace (Lk 1:79).

Forgive, and ye shall be forgiven (Lk 6:37).

Let all bitterness, and wrath, and anger, and clamour, and evil speaking, be put away from you, with all malice: and be ye kind one to another, tenderhearted, forgiving one another, even as God for Christ's sake hath forgiven you (Eph 4:31-32).

Mad Like a Forty-Four

Submit yourselves therefore to God. Resist the devil, and he will flee from you (Jas 4:7).

Back in the day, whenever a person became hot under the collar, or burning mad, my folks would say, he or she is as mad as a forty-four pistol. Now, although I was unfamiliar with any kind of firearms back then (as well as I am today) I didn't need any help figuring out that if any one person became angry enough to be compared to a pistol, that that person was pretty teed off. That means they were so angry that no one could talk them out of their hot pursuit, or stand in the way of it: Now this sounds obsessed.

Be ye angry, and sin not (Eph. 4:26).

It is my understanding that there is a holy anger, which leads to righteousness, and an anger that provokes hatred, which leads to war and destruction. In the book of Luke (Chapter 19), Jesus entered the temple, His father's dwelling place and a place of restoration for future generations, and began to drive out the merchants who were abusing the temple; turning it into a market place: buying, cheating and selling. This public display of Jesus' fury was carried out to the glory of God, not unto self, nor demonic possession: Now that, I would think, is justified.

And that they may recover themselves out of the snare of the devil, who are taken captive by him at his will (2 Tim. 2:26).

One day, after telling myself that my deliverance from angryville was only allowing me to feel like a champion whenever I felt like being carnal, I expressed this concern with the Spirit of God. With an unspoken petition to sort of slide back into my other skin, I said, "You see, she was never moved by man nor consequence because to her, that was a sign of weakness." I was proud of myself when I was in that skin, but pride made me its slave. Since God is a consuming fire, the absence of His presence opens the door to every kind of demonic activity.

That afternoon, I went to the grocery store to pick up a few things and one of the clerks bagged my groceries; it was at a store where you scan your own groceries, so her help was optional. Right afterwards, my son came along and picked up the bags that were obviously filled, but because someone else bagged them, he failed to carry away everything that belonged to us. Let me just say: that day was extremely hot. Therefore, driving back to the store was not on my 'top priority' list of things to do.

Before that time however, I thought it best to phone one of the store clerks and explain my dilemma; making known my grocery shortage, and how frustrated I was about going all the way back there and he didn't seem to care very much. In fact, he responded to me as though I was some (excuse the expression) "chicken head" who was really just trying to pull a fast one. Before I could end the conversation with him, I felt a rage within that I'll never be able to explain; a rage I had not encountered since my former self was in control. It did appear as though I was out of control; so much so, I had to talk myself into stillness. I could not believe what I was feeling, nor could I control this level of anger, and over something that seemed so trivial: Now, that I call possessed.

Catch me Lord, I believe I am falling,

and I don't know what to do.

I can hear the deceiver calling,

This rage in me is nothing new.

You, my God are my stronghold,

I put my trust in you.

O rescue me from this dark shadow,

All praise and honor give I to you.

Point of Contact

Understanding those things that work our last nerve may help us dodge frustrating situations before they occur. However, asking God to teach us how to walk after His Spirit so we do not fulfill the lust of the flesh (this includes rage) will enable us to walk through the fire without the smell of smoke.

Chapter Twenty

The Bible

*T*he law of the Lord is perfect, converting the soul: the testimony of the Lord is sure, making wise the simple (Ps. 19:7).

Thy word is a lamp unto my feet, and a light unto my path (Ps. 119:10).

It is written, That man shall not live by bread alone, but by every word of God (Lk. 4:4).

In the beginning was the Word, and the Word was with God, and the Word was God (Jn. 1:1).

The Manual

For the word of God is quick, and powerful, and sharper than any two edged sword, piercing even to the dividing asunder of soul and spirit, and of the joints and marrow, and is a discerner of the thoughts and intents of the heart (Heb. 4:12).

Isn't it amazing that we can know the thoughts, feelings, and purposes of God's heart simply by reading His word. And we, God's children may walk in victory in this life by simply following His instructions from this one book. The Bible is the most anointed book on the face of this earth, and it contains the power to loose the chains of bondage from demonic oppression, obsession, possession and depression.

It is written in 2 Timothy 3:16, "All scripture is given by inspiration of God, and is profitable for doctrine, for reproof, for correction, for instruction in righteousness: That the man of God may be perfect, thoroughly furnished unto all good works." Now do you know that while a number of persons are rejoicing over this good news, others are scoffing at it and denying the power of such a statement?

One morning while visiting relatives, I opened my Bible to read a couple of verses of scripture (which is a very edifying thing to do). But then, before I was able to do so, a relative asked, "What do you want to read that for?" I was shocked to the point of silence and wondered if my timing was wrong. You know, perhaps there's a particular time and place for reading God's instruction book.

Really, I felt humiliated and even somewhat out of place, as I struggled to reason out what in the world could possibly be wrong with reading a book that does not contain derogatory words or phrases? How is it that I felt insulted and yet I was made out of the image and likeness of a Mighty God. But wait a minute!"

For this person, it seemed that much time had gone by and they appeared to be lonely and lost at times. In fact, they were downright miserable; but no doubt this way of life was a okay. As I continued to search for a passage of scripture, this person quickly slipped away and after a little while returned. This person then threw a book on my lap as if to say, "Here's a book, read this one since you care to get that deep." I was appalled, but managed to retain my decorum in the light of the situation.

Okay, so you would prefer to read about romance. Well, try reading the book of Ruth. There you'll witness a truly romantic relationship between a man a woman, one with a truly happy ending that refreshes the imagination. Or maybe you like drama, with a little bad boy stuff; then read some of the books in the Old Testament, and there you'll come face to face with conflicting events. No wait, you like poetry! Well, open the book to Song of Solomon and become truly fascinated with the art of poetry in motion. Worldly events? Then spend some time reading the books of Daniel and Revelation, and you'll be amazed to learn that the end is closer than you might think.

There you have it: From love and romance, to freedom and parental guidance, and so much more: All from this one book.

The Bible is God's cure for the common life.

Point of Contact

Check out the Bible on tape or CD while relaxing, exercising or driving. However, if you're still a bit puzzled, check out a child's Bible. I've discovered that simple analogies that are self-explanatory make learning the Word fun.

Revelation Knowledge

But whom say ye that I am? And Simon Peter answered and said, Thou art the Christ, the Son of the Living God. And Jesus answered and said unto him, Blessed art thou, Simon Bar-jona: for flesh and blood hath not revealed it unto thee, but My Father which is in heaven (Mt. 16:15-17).

Eye hath not seen, nor ear heard, neither have entered into the heart of man, the things which God hath prepared for them that love Him. But God hath revealed them unto us by His Spirit: for the Spirit searcheth all things, yea, the deep things of God (1Cor. 2:9-10).

For what man knoweth the things of a man, save the spirit of man which is in him? even so the things of God knoweth no man, but the Spirit of God. Now we have received, not the spirit of the world, but the spirit which is of God; that we might know the things that are freely given to us of God (1 Cor. 2:11-12).

But the natural man receiveth not the things of the Spirit of God: for they are foolishness unto him: neither can he know them, because they are spiritually discerned (1 Cor. 2:14).

When God Whispers

But God hath revealed them unto us by His Spirit: for the Spirit searcheth all things, yea, the deep things of God (1 Cor. 2:10).

Nowadays most people laugh at anyone who says, "God spoke to me!" No doubt, anyone who God speaks to is absolutely crazy to the carnally minded. But all things considered, if you were given the privilege and the power to create the human race, would you provide no form of communication between the created and their creator?

Of course, not! So why would it be impossible for God's Spirit who dwells on the inside of every believer to communicate with His own – even on our own faith level?

"Look girly! You might answer, that's too much drama, let's just call it intuition, and be done with it."

Intuition? You mean a hunch? Well, since God is all-knowing, whenever He reveals anything to a child of His, there is no guesswork, nor error.

One day while at home, just doing simple little things in the kitchen, a still small voice said to me, "Your sister is pregnant, but no one knows it." Actually, it was to early for her to even assume pregnancy, but the still small voice continued, "Whenever she learns of her pregnancy, she will not wish to share the news with you for fear of upsetting you." I paused for a second to consider the goodness of God and how He cares about those things that concern us.

You see, I had recently experienced a miscarriage. Therefore, my sister's decision in not wanting to share this news with me would have been quite understandable. Still, it would have been more painful for me to think that such wonderful news could not touch my ears because of a minor setback. So I thanked the messenger with the still small voice for His gracious kindness.

Later on that week, I decided to give my sister a call and chat with her a bit. Through casual conversation, I shared with her the wonderful news that was given to me by the "still small voice" but it did not seem likely, not to her knowledge anyway. However, a month later I went home to visit the folks and stopped over at my sister's home, there she greeted me excitedly and shared the news of her pregnancy. Her joy at that moment knew no bounds and I was thrilled to think that the messenger with the still small voice would share with me those wonderful things that God alone knows.

Point of Contact

Prayer puts us in a position to hear and recognize the still small voice of God. Spend a few minutes each day talking to the Father that you may become sensitive to His still small voice.

Victory

Nay, in all these things we are more than conquerors through Him that loved us. For I am persuaded, that neither death, nor life, nor angels, nor principalities, nor powers, nor things present, nor things to come, Nor height, nor depth, nor any other creature, shall be able to separate us from the love of God, which is in Christ Jesus our Lord (Rom. 8:37-38).

For the scripture saith, Whosoever believeth on Him shall not be ashamed (Rom. 10:11).

The sting of death is sin; and the strength of sin is the law. But thanks be to God, which giveth us the victory through our Lord Jesus Christ (1 Cor. 15: 56-57).

And they overcame Him by the blood of the Lamb, and by the word of their testimony; and they love not their lives unto death (Rev. 12:11).

The Last Laugh

Whosoever believeth that Jesus is the Christ is born of God: and every one that loveth Him that begat loveth Him also that is begotten of Him. By this we know that we love the children of God, when we love God, and keep His commandments. For this is the love of God, that we keep His commandments: and His commandments are not grievous. For whatsoever is born of God overcometh the world: and this is the victory that overcometh the world, even our faith (1 Jn. 5:1-5).

"I believe, I believe, I know it sounds funny but I believe!" These words may not make you a part of the world's clique and it surely will not make you well favored where old Satan is concerned, but after you've received Him, though your battles must continue, consider yourself royalty. That's right, you're an overcomer, the child of the King – not a king, but the King.

When the world was young, and things were becoming way out of hand, and the poor children of God cried out to Him, He knew that the only thing to do was to send a mediator – someone who could stand up for man in His sight and be counted as a spotless lamb. As God the Father thought on these things, He knew of one Person, and one Person alone who fit that description perfectly. "My Son," He thought, "My precious, precious Son." And, I imagine it went this way:

One day, while walking down the corridors of heaven, Jesus, the Son of God, noticed His Father standing towards a vast window with His head bowed down, as if looking at His feet. He, Jesus was concerned to see His Father this way, knowing His Father as El-Elyon – the most High God, could fix anything at a spoken word, or a simple glance. Suddenly, He walked into the great room where His Father was standing, and after getting His attention said, "Father, what is it? What could possibly be the matter? Tell me, and I will help you fix it." His father looked up at him with sadden eyes, and began telling him of man's coming destruction. "They have no one," He said, "no one can save them from what lies ahead in the very near future."

"Son," He continued, "they will be destroyed. Satan is having a field day right now, this is certain."

Without another word, the Father stared into His Son's eyes and Jesus knew what He must do. He was not overzealous upon hearing of the great commission; after all, being a mediator is a real tough job, and He soon learned that He would have hell to pay for simply, well as old Satan would put it, "rescuing a bunch of hell-bounders." But, instead of faltering under the weight, this Jesus dethroned Himself and stepped into the womb of a virgin, became man, performed ultimate miracles of every kind, suffered, died, was buried, and then entered hell's gates to take away the keys of death and destruction from old Satan himself. Then returning to His Father on that day of His Ascension he said, "Now Father, I have not lost one of these that belongs to you."

I don't know about you, but just knowing that He came to earth, suffered and died for me is all the reason for me to not only give Him my life, but to stand up and cheer for this man Jesus.

Yes! I believe, I believe, it may sound funny, but I believe.

Point of Contact

Fifteen minutes a day in God's Word helps me understand my inheritance and walk in victory.

Wisdom

And God gave Solomon wisdom and understanding exceeding much, and largeness of heart, even as the sand that is on the seashore (1 Kin. 4:29).

The fear of the Lord is the beginning of wisdom: and good understanding have all they that do His commandments: His praise endureth for ever (Ps. 111:10).

So that thou incline thine ear unto wisdom, and apply thine heart to understanding; yea, if thou criest after knowledge, and liftest up thy voice for understanding; if thou seekest her as silver, and searchest for her as for hid treasures; then shalt thou understand the fear of the Lord, and find the knowledge of God (Prov. 2:2-5).

The Gift of Solomon

And now, O Lord my God, Thou hast made Thy servant King instead of David my father: and I am but a little child: I know not how to go out or come in (1 Kin. 3:7).

What makes a person wise? Is it brash words eloquently spoken, or drawing near to God and His word, obeying the laws of wisdom? In the book of Kings, Solomon asked God for the gift that mattered most to him: wisdom. According to the word of God, Solomon walked in the favor of the Lord and therefore, he could have asked for anything; he chose wisdom.

I would imagine wisdom to be the one gift that we all need to live a successful life. Surely, our leaders in governing, presidential and civil offices would make a world of difference if they were to seek the face of God and ask Him for this special gift. Indeed, God would be pleased to give it freely, for it is written, "If any of you lack wisdom, let him ask of God that giveth to all men liberally, and upbraideth not: and it shall be given him" (Jas. 1:5).

Think about it. This one gift from God could possibly help us make the right career move and as a result, we would waste no time wandering or wondering. There would be no faulty marriages or unnecessary debts. You know, the world's idea of wisdom comes with high-sounding words and clanging noises, forever figuring out get rich quick schemes, then trampling down those less fortunate ones. However, whenever Solomon asked God for wisdom, God knew that he could be trusted with riches as well. Therefore, ask God for wisdom, for though you've not been chosen to rule the country, you'll operate richly in the world around you.

Point of Contact

I enjoy spending time listening to people who speak wisely. Still, I've come to understand that the only way to get wisdom is to ask God for it.

Chapter Twenty-One

Abuse

*T*he Spirit of the Lord is upon Me, because He hath anointed Me to preach the gospel to the poor, He hath sent Me to heal the brokenhearted, to preach deliverance to the captives, and recovery of sight to the blind, to set at liberty them that are bruised, To preach the acceptable year of the Lord (Lk. 4:18-19).

Woman, thou art loosed from thine infirmity (Lk. 13:12).

For the law of the Spirit of life in Christ Jesus hath made me free from the law of sin and death (Rom. 8:2).

For our light affliction, which is but for a moment, worketh for us a far more exceeding and eternal weight of glory (2 Cor. 4:17).

Beauty and the Beast

For we wrestle not against flesh and blood, but against principalities, against powers, against the rulers of the darkness of this world, against spiritual wickedness in high places (Eph. 6:12).

I've never been a victim of physical abuse and from what I hear, I pray that I never become one. After all, my own dad whom God had given the rights to discipline his own with the rod, never lifted a hand to strike my three sisters or myself; with this I find abusive behavior deplorable.

In essence, anyone, either male or female can become the victim of one form of abuse or another; many were victimized as children. No doubt, for some, this makes up the perfect excuse for which their conscience rests. However, before we choose to make our past the guidepost that directs our future, perhaps we might consider this verse of scripture: "For from within, out of the heart of men, proceed evil thoughts, adulteries, fornication, murders, thefts, covetousness, wickedness, deceit, lasciviousness, an evil eye, blasphemy, pride, foolishness: all these evil things come from within, and defile the man (Mk. 7:21-23).

One day, as I was driving home from work, a man stepped out of his vehicle while the light was red, walked over to my car, then angrily hit against my window on the driver's side with his hand. I was startled! I actually jumped at how much he startled me. I then wondered what I did to enrage him. You see as it was, he and I were in two different lanes, so it could not have been road rage. Besides, it was very early in the morning when drivers are scarce. Suddenly, I turned towards my window and glanced at this creature neatly dressed in black and white with crystal blue eyes and jet black hair, pushed back as to accentuate his already distinguished features.

He wore a smirk, camouflaged behind his all too sophisticated looking demeanor, as if his disgusting behavior pleased him to the highest, or at least the one by whom he was being used. As I continued on my way home, still shaken up by such obnoxious behavior, my thoughts centered primarily on that man, and immediately, I realized that my battle, however short-lived was not with that man... not really. For no matter what his reasons were for openly displaying whatever issues he was dealing with from within, my real battle was with the devil.

Look! I realize that many of us suffer from an inferiority complex, which can lead to fear, anger, then perhaps, violent behavior; but as it stands: "the devil's purpose is to kill, steal and destroy" (Jn. 10:10).

Point of Contact

Enough is enough! Since God wants His children, (that includes you) to live in peace, make a decision to go after peace. In some cases, bondage is deep rooted; still, God did not give us a spirit of fear, but of power, love and a sound mind (2 Tim. 1:7).

Attitude

All the days of my appointed time will I wait, till my change comes (Job 14:14).

And be renewed in the spirit of your mind; and that ye put on the new man, which after God is created in righteousness and true holiness (Eph. 4:23-24).

For ye are dead, and your life is hid with Christ with God (Col. 3:3).

But now ye also put off all these; anger, wrath, malice, blasphemy, filthy communication out of your mouth. Lie not one to another, seeing that ye have put off the old man with his deeds; And have put on the new man, which is renewed in knowledge after the image of Him that created you (Col. 3:8-10).

I Stand Accused

For if we would judge ourselves, we should not be judged (1 Cor. 11:31).

"Mirror, mirror on the wall: who's the nastiest of them all?"

Someone said that having a good attitude is more important than schooling, wealth, situations, disappointments and achievements. It is more important than looks, aptitude or power. Therefore, having a good attitude, even in the midst of foolishness and misunderstanding, can produce seeds of goodness in us.

When I was growing up, I was easily offended and whenever that happened, my attitude would change drastically. In other words, I'd become a totally different person. Like anyone else, I'd flow with the wind whenever things were going according to plan, or the way I wanted them to. But, sometimes when I was exposed to some other minor occurrences, usually caused by those around me, I'd dig a hole and hide for a while, then come out with a pistol and holster.

My mom, being baffled by my Dr. Jekyll/Mr. Hyde personality, would say to me, "Sylvia, you remind me of a snake!" (speaking in reference to the shedding of his skin). I didn't understand at the time, however, as time progressed, through trial and error, I learned of this side of me that I'd grown to love.

I love the way God cares for me, and leads me to Himself like a gentle shepherd. You know, every now and then, whenever I step into my old self, I go to my mirror and begin to judge my attitude concerning the issues of the day. Did I present my case in love, or was I unapologetic to someone in authority, I ask myself while standing before my mirror, did you purposely overlook that wandering soul today? Many times, I am ashamed of what I refuse to do simply because my carnal self said not to, and I wonder what God thinks.

There He stands, the just Judge in His chambers, awaiting the prosecution of those who perhaps, had grown into "hard to handle" individuals, or those with the "I'll do it my way" syndrome. Indeed, there is judgment awaiting every individual. A judgment where we all will stand before the just judge and listen in silence as He makes known to us our attitude towards Him, whether we realized our dependence on Him or not. He'll want to know, I'm sure, about our attitude towards those who mourned. Were we compassionate enough to mourn with them?

Or, consider our attitude towards the little "insignificant" people: Did we lend an ear to their cry? Then He'll say, "Tell me, what was your reaction to those who were hungry, even thirsty, for justice and mercy? Did you scorn those with pure hearts, or persecute My chosen ones, because they chose to live for Me?" While standing there with heads bowed down, most of us will say, "Forgive me, Lord, for my unsightly attitude while I was on the earth. I have no excuse; I stand accused."

Point of Contact

Choose to change! Being around a person with a bad attitude disrupts a peaceful environment.

Loneliness

And the Lord God said, "It is not good that the man should be alone; I will make him an help meet for him" (Gen. 2:18).

God setteth the solitary in families: He bringeth out those which are bound with chains (Ps. 68:6).

Two are better than one; because they have a good reward for their labour (Eccl. 4:9).

And, lo, I am with you always, even unto the end of the world. Amen (Mt. 28:20).

Who Lives Alone

A man that hath friends must show himself friendly: and there is a friend that sticketh closer than a brother (Prov. 18:24).

For a season, my grandmother, who recently went home to be with the Lord, lived alone for quite some time before moving in with her son and his family. Before that time however, during one of my visits to see her, she greeted me excitedly, as though seeing me brought back memories of long ago. I too was delighted knowing that my visit to her home would make her day, and that it gave me the pleasure of collecting some of those old memories of yesterday to tuck away in my heart.

Once I sat down, she began to express feelings of emptiness, and from the expression on her face, it was clear to see that loneliness was eating away at her. You know, it isn't hard to think back on those days of yesteryear, when family was all around, and a few grandchildren were busy playing in the backyard. Meanwhile others pulled at grandmother's apron for something delicious she'd baked several minutes ago.

How quickly those years seem to roll by and suddenly you find yourself all alone wishing those days would come back again, if only for a little while. Why, sometimes you rehearse them in the back of your mind for so long until you could almost hear the sound of laughter from those grandchildren in the backyard, family members coming and going, and even feel those little hands pulling on your apron. Life is funny that way, isn't it?

But, since we're not promised permanent years on this earth or lasting happiness, the Lord God decided long ago to wrap Himself up in a cloak of flesh and step down into the womb of a virgin. He came to live a life of one who understands our pangs of loneliness, and choose to be to us a friend who sticks closer than any family member does.

He is a friend that your soul will never outgrow. He's the same yesterday, today and forevermore (Heb. 13:8). His presence still renews old things: welcome His Spirit in your life today.

Point of Contact

Commit yourself to being a friend, that you might have a friend. Give your time to others, even those who may not be a part of your clique; then live, love and laugh.

Sorrow

For this day is holy unto our Lord: neither be ye sorry; for the joy of the Lord is your strength (Neh. 8:10).

Weeping may endure for a night, but joy cometh in the morning (Ps. 30:5).

A merry heart doeth good like a medicine: but a broken spirit drieth the bones (Prov. 17:22).

And the ransomed of the Lord shall return, and come to Zion with songs and everlasting joy upon their heads: they shall obtain joy and gladness, and sorrow and sighing shall flee away (Is. 35:10).

For I will turn their mourning into joy, and will comfort them, and make them rejoice from their sorrow (Jer. 31:13).

For I have satiated the weary soul, and I have replenished every sorrowful soul (Jer. 31:25).

Blessed are they that mourn: for they shall be comforted (Mt. 5:4).

Thorn in the Flesh

To appoint unto them that mourn in Zion, to give unto them beauty for ashes, the oil of joy for mourning, the garment of praise for the spirit of heaviness (Is. 61:3).

Whenever I'm feeling sorrowful, I turn to the Lord, my solid rock. Let's face it! Sorrow is no stranger to anyone: all have experienced it at some time in this life. But, like Job, God's is always ready to walk with us through the process– not necessarily out of it.

Years ago, I discovered that I was pregnant for the second time. I was thrilled! I was familiar with the truth that children are a gift from the Lord, therefore my excitement knew no bounds. However, before I could purchase any maternity clothing, or buy a pair of baby booties I miscarried. Without warning, my hopes of cuddling another baby in my arms were lost between anticipation and chance.

Still, as it were (and this sounds awkward) my outlook on the matter fluctuated. My emotions went from disappointment to contentment, and although I could not believe that such an ordeal had happened to me, I knew that God was watching over all that concerned me.

Naturally speaking, the loss of a child, whether existing in or out of the womb, can be an emotional experience that can weigh your spirit down heavily while raging hormones are also of no help. But, when I could no longer carry the weight of such a burden, I cried out to my God, Jehovah Rapha – my healer; the one who makes bitter experiences sweet. While standing alone in my room, I recall the hush from the background that gave ear to a pin drop; even the tears that quickly fell to my feet. All of a sudden, I heard His still calm voice say: "Go to her, she's in distress!" At once, God's breath of peace (not some hormonal balance), filled my heart and made quiet the disturbance in my mind, and I was instantly made whole.

On the real side: I'll tell you that the Lord did not restore that which I had lost in the natural. He soon showed me that He had other plans. However, He did restore my body, mind and spirit, enabling me to walk through the sorrow with hope as immediately as I would have liked.

But look! There are many things in this life that will bring about sorrow. A sick child, for instance, a divorce, a diseased body, the loss of a spouse, or division among the body of Christ. But, I praise God that the chastisement of our peace was upon Him some two thousand years ago, and with His stripes, we are healed... body, soul and spirit.

Point of Contact

Everyone needs time alone, time to regroup, even if it's only for a short time. Starve your sorrowing soul with relaxing music, a walk in the park, even a moment to cry. Now, sing hymns of praise, even if you really don't feel like it. No! It's no magic potion for relieving the pain and sorrow, but it does invite God's Spirit to lift that spirit of heaviness.

Chapter Twenty-Two

Foolishness

*F*or when we were in the flesh, the motions of sins, which were by the law, did work in our members to bring forth fruit unto death. But now we are delivered from the law, that being dead wherein we were held; that we should serve in newness of spirit, and not in the oldness of the letter (Rom. 7:5-6).

For the good that I would I do not: but the evil which I would not, that I do (Rom. 7:19).

For they that are after the flesh do mind the things of the flesh; but they that are after the Spirit the things of the Spirit (Rom. 8:5).

For if ye live after the flesh, ye shall die: but if ye through the Spirit do mortify the deeds of the body, ye shall live (Rom. 8:13).

Fools of Folly

As a dog returneth to his vomit, so a fool returneth to his folly (Prov. 26:11).

Think about this: Would you thrust a knife in the wound of and injured person? Or, perhaps, send a sick child out in the cold? Of course, not; that would be almost inhuman. Then why is it, we do not realize that a person suffering from an addiction to alcohol, whether they realize it or not, is an ill person? And, why is it that we tend to offer them a drink, rather than laugh at their vile behavior afterwards? My mother once said, "Have you ever noticed that upon visiting folks how quickly they offer you a drink rather than a simple cup of coffee."

A relative of mine once approached me quite boldly and pulled his wallet out of his pocket to ask if I would participate in his attempt to feed an old illness. You see the abuse of alcohol was no stranger to him; in fact the addiction itself had opened the door to a generation of followers. Nevertheless, at that moment, I felt intimidated by his boldness, and instantly nodded yes to his request. However, in a split second, the Spirit of God rebuked the spirit of intimidation in me and strengthened my weakness. Afterwards, I repented, then kindly refused to be a part of the very thing that holds those in bondage.

Point of Contact

Tradition plays a very important role in keeping us tied to those things that open the door to foolishness, in order to keep us from those things that we have grown accustomed to. I feel my way around people and their way of living, then I find the balance.

Lust

I speak after the manner of men because of the infirmity of your flesh: for as ye have yielded your members servants to uncleanness and to iniquity; even so now yield your members servants to righteousness unto holiness (Rom. 6:19).

For when ye were the servants of sin, ye were free from righteousness. What fruit had ye then in those things where of ye are now ashamed? For the end of those things is death (Rom. 6:20-21).

And be not conformed to this world: but be ye transformed by the renewing of your mind, that ye may prove what is that good, and acceptable, and perfect will of God (Rom. 12:2).

Ye are of God, little children, and have overcome them: because greater is He that is in you, than he that is in the world (1 Jn. 4:4).

Crucified

I am crucified with Christ: nevertheless I live; yet not I, but Christ liveth in me: and the life which I now live in the flesh I live by the faith of the Son of God, who loved me, and gave Himself for me (Gal. 2:20).

If there were a spiritual formula to control lustful addictions, I would imagine it to be as simple as this: "Put them to death!" Lust in itself is a never satisfied addiction, and though it operates through many different facets, the lust of the flesh through sexual uncleanness casts a dark shadow.

Do you know that a Christian, one who has given their heart to the Lord, even after asking God to forgive them of sin, can fall under the persuasion of the enemy and become hopelessly addicted to lust? However, if we control that which we see, hear and entertain, we may walk triumphantly in the fight.

Some years ago, a co-worker handed me a book that she'd spent time reading and said how wonderful it was; I don't recall the title, but judging from the contents I should have handed it right back to her. Instead, I was drawn by curiosity and decided to read at least a few chapters of this bewitching, provocative thriller. Well, not long after, I became a victim in a battle of the flesh, unknowingly; the invitation was made simple through words in a book by a spirit who, perhaps, guided the author.

Although, I labored in prayer concerning this stronghold, I was unable to free myself from such bondage; but through the power of touching and agreeing with a prayer warrior, I was set free and made to walk in victory.

How simple it is for the adversary, the devil, to set the plot; we being simple take the bait, and set ourselves up for destruction.

Point of Contact

Separate yourself from those things that are meant to lead you into sin. Remember, the flesh is like a spoiled child, so get serious.

———

Sex

To everything there is a season, and a time to every purpose under the heaven (Eccl. 3:1).

He hath made every thing beautiful in His time (Eccl. 3:11).

I charge you, O ye daughters of Jerusalem, by the roes, and by the hinds of the field, that ye stir not up, nor awake my love, till he pleases (Song 3:5).

I beseech you therefore, brethren, by the mercies of God, that ye present your bodies a living sacrifice, holy, acceptable unto God, which is your reasonable service (Rom. 12:1).

And be not conformed to this world: but be ye transformed by the renewing of your mind, that ye may prove what is that good, and acceptable, and perfect will of God (Rom. 12:2).

Marriage is honorable in all, and the bed undefiled: but whoremongers and adulterers God will judge (Heb. 13:4).

That Three Letter Word

And God saw everything that He had made, and, behold, it was very good (Gen. 1:31).

Whenever my mom wanted to talk about sex, she would say "you know, that three-letter word." So, I thought it honorable to entitle this as the "Shh... Three-Letter Word." Believe it or not, for some of us, sex is a dishonorable thing. Folks, who perhaps were forced to submit to an act that should have been romantically enticed, now carry the weight of bondage and shame. Worse yet, this same spirit fell on those of a different generation who are yet knowledgeable concerning the truth. May God's Spirit of peace and wholeness settle within your heart.

Now, let us not forget to talk about sex, c'mon now. Remember: God made sex and He made it good. We know this from scripture, and our natural senses can identify to this truth. However, like money, sex in itself isn't evil; it's the addiction to it that is at the root of evil. Indeed, it can be difficult for some of us to take control of our lower nature and bring under subjection those powerful, untimely desires, but God always provides a way of escape whenever we are tempted beyond what we are able to bear.

I was a teenager whenever I discovered this stirring of the emotions and, naturally speaking, it was difficult for me to put the whole thing into it's proper prospective. Therefore, I got alone with God in my prayer closet and outlined my thoughts and even my frustrations concerning something that I could hardly understand, much less control. Whenever I finished laying the matter at the Lord's feet, I felt assured that He would guide me through it all. Now, do you know that in order for me to receive God's supernatural blessing, I had to line myself up with His commands? That's right! You see God was not responsible for that which I allowed to take hold of my senses; therefore, it was necessary for me to guard my senses through obedience to His word.

Did I hear you say, "How can a young person stay pure?" By being honest with God and yourself, and keeping the channels of communication opened.

Point of Contact

Since sex is beautiful thing to God. We should be ashamed of condemning ourselves for an act that He preordained before the foundations of the world. However, since sex out-of-order is offensive to God, we should be ashamed of the act and repent. Listen! If this stirring of the emotions is a bit more than you can stand, do not try an act pious: simply ask the Holy Spirit to remove it for the time being. Don't worry, like a bee returns to the comb, the rousing will surely return.

The Tongue

Thou shalt also decree a thing, and it shall be established unto thee (Job 22:28).

I said, I will take heed to my ways, that I sin not with my tongue: I will keep my mouth with a bridle, while the wicked is before me (Ps. 39:1).

Set a watch, O Lord, before my mouth; keep the door of my lips (Ps. 141:3).

Hear; for I will speak of excellent things; and the opening of my lips shall be right things. For my mouth shall speak truth; and wickedness is an abomination to my lips. All the words of my mouth are in righteousness; there is nothing forward or perverse in them (Prov. 8:6-8).

There is that speaketh like the piercings of a sword: but the tongue of the wise is health (Prov. 12:18).

If any man among you seem to be religious, and bridleth not his tongue, but deceiveth his own heart, this man's religion is vain (Jas. 1:26).

Satan's Mouthpiece

And the tongue is a fire, a world of iniquity: so is the tongue among our members that it defileth the whole body, and setteth on fire the course of nature; and it is set on fire of hell (Jas. 3:6).

When we were growing up, my mother would advise us against speaking foolishly– that is, speaking before thinking. No, she did not recall the verse of scripture in James 3:6, informing us that our words would eventually determine our course in life. Nor did she consider the verse of scripture in Proverbs 18:21, informing us that we could very well put to death the actual thing for which we were trusting God through the simple use of the tongue.

But, this one thing she did know: the tongue could be used as a mouthpiece for Satan. No doubt, his secret plan is that we become our own worse enemy by unconstructive words.

Say What?

Do you know that the tongue as a mouthpiece for Satan can deposit ungodly seeds in a marriage, where a spirit of division upsets the balance of harmony and love between a husband and a wife? Wait, there's more. The tongue as a mouthpiece for Satan can destroy all hopes of a child's desire for achievement.

The tongue as a mouthpiece for Satan can stop the miracle-working power of God over your blessing, canceling the manifestation of it in the natural realm. The tongue as a mouthpiece for Satan can ignite a flame of anger that burns and causes much destruction. The tongue as a mouthpiece for Satan, opens the door to negative mind games that may invite sickness and disease, causing the word of God concerning your healing to be of no affect.

Now know this: "Death and life are in the power of the tongue and they that love it shall eat the fruit thereof" (Prov. 18:21).

Point of Contact

The Bible says that God's word does not return to Him void (Is. 55:11). Therefore, decree restoration of health to your body, speak peace and prosperity over your children each day. Then get up off your patty wagon and seek after those things that you are professing.

———————————

Addiction

I beseech you therefore, brethren, by the mercies of God, that ye present your bodies a living sacrifice, holy, acceptable unto God, which is your reasonable service (Rom. 12:1).

And be not conformed to this world: but be ye transformed by the renewing of your mind, that ye may prove what is that good, and acceptable, and perfect will of God (Rom. 12:2).

Put on the whole armour of God, that ye may be able to stand against the wiles of the devil (Eph. 6:11).

Greater is He that is in me than he that is in the world (1 Jn. 4:4).

Sanctify them through Thy truth: Thy word is truth (Jn. 17:17).

Insatiable

Purge me with hyssop, and I shall be clean: wash me, and I shall be whiter than snow. Create in me a clean heart, O God; and renew a right spirit within me (Ps. 51:7-10).

Her husband had been ill for quite some time. However, his illness was not induced by any physical infirmity that would afflict a certain area of his body. No! His ache went far beyond what modern medicine could cure.

One day, Jane Doe (as I will call her) and I met after our workday was done and the two of us decided to stop off at a little restaurant to get a bite to eat. While sitting there, I carefully observed a very meticulous individual, who, in my opinion, was always nicely put together. However, today, she was unlike her usual self, her once dazzling smile appeared distorted, as though formed by hardened clay. Her warm gentle spirit seemed cast down, and the radiance of her well made-up face appeared to be masked with complexity. Although she tried her best to portray her usual, well put together self, it was clear to see that her pain went beyond anything, anyone in the cosmetic industry could patent.

"Talk to me girl," I said, "tell me what's on your mind. Perhaps I can help to bring some closure to whatever it is that's bothering you."

She nodded. Then, with hesitation, began telling me of her husband's addiction to virtual adultery.

"Pornography?" I said.

"Yes!" She continued, "I don't really know what to do, 'cause you know how these things are – one obsession almost, always leads to another and there's just too much rivalry. I feel hopeless."

I sat there seemingly still, wanting to say, "Look, why don't you let him know how you feel, then put some emphasis on separation if the matter isn't resolved in due time." But then, I felt a nudge way down in the pit of my being to keep a lid on that thought. Instead, however, I said, "Look, as Christians, you and I both know the old phrase: 'Christ is the answer!' Isn't just a phrase – it's fact. If I might make a suggestion to the part of you that understands victory: 'Try God!' I mean really try God. Spend time in prayer, even fasting, that He might lead you into peace as well as victory."

She smiled and said, "Well, that sounds like a plan to me, besides the tears are wearing me out and reversing my facials – if you know what I mean."

Days turned into weeks before the two of us had any real time to talk to one another. Then one day she phoned me and said, "You'll never guess what I learned? Even after days of fasting and praying, I returned to my little corner of the world, upset about the matter that appeared unresolved. But, while sitting there, in the midst of one of my tearful episodes, the Lord spoke very gently to me saying, "Why are you so upset? You're not the one with the problem." Instantly, I was delivered from what I learned as bondage in a place called Egypt." "Now," she continued, "I'm learning how to lift myself up in prayer, along with counseling, that I might be healed of the pain of rejection and with it strength to overcome the pain of an unhealthy situation."

Point of Contact

Bless me Father for I have sinned; forgive me Father for through you I find real forgiveness. Heal me Father, for your healing brings purity. Restore me Father, and make me willing to serve you. Sometimes certain addictions derive from generational curses; if that is the case, seek help, perhaps from a reliable pastor, one who is Word-minded. Then ask God to help you every step of the way.

Chapter Twenty-Three

Sin

*T*hat which I see not teach Thou me: if I have done iniquity, I will do no more (Job 34:32).

Let not sin therefore reign in your mortal body, that ye should obey it in the lust thereof (Rom. 6:12).

For the wages of sin is death; but the gift of God is eternal life through Jesus Christ our Lord (Rom. 6:23).

Neither yield ye your members as instruments of unrighteousness unto sin: but yield yourselves unto God, as those that are alive from the dead, and your members as instruments of righteousness unto God for sin shall not have dominion over you: for ye are not under the law, but under grace (Rom. 6:13-14).

Crimson

Come now, and let us reason together, saith the Lord: though your sins be as scarlet, they shall be as white as snow; though they be red like crimson, they shall be as wool (Is. 1:18).

Have you ever discovered a terrible stain on a nice piece of clothing that you simply loved and no matter how hard you tried to remove the stain, it simply would not come out? In the end, did you decide that it was not worth the trouble, so you went out to find something nice to try to replace the former piece of clothing?

Well, do you know that our sin to God is like that terrible stain on that nice piece of clothing? But, even though God hates the sin, He loves us, His children, no matter what. Indeed, God managed to send down prophets and the like to help us realize the ugliness of sin, but not one could wash that stain away. In other words, we would have been stained for life; yes even tossed out, hell bound. But God in His great love, mercy, and wisdom sent to earth the only stain removing, sin-rebuking man who could put to death sin's ability to destroy God's nice piece of work.

Jesus Christ, the Holy Son of God destroyed the power of sin over our lives, therefore we have the power to resist the world, the flesh, and the devil, and say no to sin.

Point of Contact

You know, even if we never confess a single sin to God, it won't make the sin less visible to Him. So come on, get it off your chest. Surely He won't love you any less. On the contrary, I would think that our confession draws Him closer.

Strife

A wrathful man stirreth up strife: but he that is slow to anger appeaseth strife (Prov. 15:18).

The beginning of strife is as when one letteth out water: therefore leave off contention, before it be meddled with (Prov. 17:14).

It is an honour for a man to cease from strife; but every fool will be meddling (Prov. 20:3).

Where no wood is, there the fire goeth out: so where there is no talebearer, the strife ceaseth (Prov. 26:20).

Let nothing be done through strife or vainglory; but in lowliness of mind let each esteem other better than themselves (Phil. 2:3).

For where envying and strife is, there is confusion and every evil work (Jas. 3:16).

Be still, and know that I am God (Ps. 46:10a).

What Jesus Did

Let all bitterness, and wrath, and anger, and clamour, and evil speaking, be put away from you, with all malice: and be ye kind one to another tenderhearted, forgiving one another, even as God for Christ's sake hath forgiven you (Eph. 4:31-32).

Surely, most of us have taken notice of the ever-popular inquiry: "What would Jesus do?" On the contrary, I've often asked myself this question whenever I'm harboring feelings of anger that lead to strife, hoping perhaps that my thoughts might automatically line up with Jesus' way of thinking. But, this is not so, because having the mind of Christ does take effort on my part.

Back in the day, I was unpredictable, moody, and downright fussy, and well, to some degree, I still am all of those things. However, recently, through the conviction and leading of the Holy Spirit, I'm learning how to deal with this weakness of the flesh and do what Jesus would do in given situations and forfeit my rights. Sounds passive doesn't it?

But it isn't! Because whenever you choose the way of peace, you invite the Lord to take the entire matter in His hands; in other words, the battle becomes His. However, unlike Jesus, I may discover that I am wrong and have no rights at all. At this point I turn to the Spirit of God that He might make all things right. Surely this takes faith, but whatever you do, do not allow the spirit of strife through anger, self-pity, and slander in, because believe me, it's a spiritual crippler.

Point of Contact

Go after peace! True, some people are hard to get along with and those kinds of people will test you. Without being overly passive, turn the other cheek and put the matter in the hand of God where it is always resolved peaceably.

Temptation

But God is faithful, who will not suffer you to be tempted above that ye are able; but will with the temptation also make a way to escape, that ye may be able to bear it (1 Cor. 10:13).

For in that He Himself hath suffered being tempted, He is able to succour them that are tempted (Heb. 2:18).

For we have not an High Priest which cannot be touched with the feeling of our infirmities; but was in all points tempted like as we are, yet without sin (Heb. 4:15).

Let no man say when he is tempted, I am tempted of God: for God cannot be tempted with evil, neither tempteth He any man: But every man is tempted, when he is drawn away of his own lust, an enticed (Jas. 1:13-14).

Things That Make You Go Hum

...Behold, Satan hath desired to have you, that he may sift you as wheat: But I have prayed for thee, that thy faith fail not: and when thou art converted, strengthen thy brethren (Lk. 22:31-32).

"Little pig, little pig, let me come in. Not by the hairs of my chinny-chin-chin! Then I'll huff, and I'll puff and I'll blow your mind."
–Satan

Do you know that the devil has a way with words? But, even so, he cannot make you do anything that you do not want to do. However, he is very cunning if you are not careful; he'll persuade you to test God, then leave you to shame and despair. That's exactly what happened to Adam and Eve so listen, as the story unfolds....

"Hum!" uttered the serpent, as he slithered his way around the garden, checking out every seed-bearing tree that adorned the surroundings. Then while gazing at one other tree, he murmured, "Hum, to die for!"

A little while later, after it dawned on him that if he used just the right amount of persuading, he could possibly make history. So he eased his way under a shaded tree, and waited.

One day, while eavesdropping, the serpent heard God instruct the man, Adam, concerning the importance of obedience. "Of any fruit in the garden thou mayest freely eat: But of the tree of the knowledge of good and evil, thou shall not eat of it: for in the day that thou eatest thereof thou shalt surely die" (Gen. 2:16-17).

Now the serpent being shrewd, instantly conjured up a scheme, because you see, he found it utterly impossible to pass up a chance to test fate. So one day, after studying both Adam and his all too curious wife Eve, the serpent sashayed himself near a tree where the woman stood, soaking up the sun.

Narrator: "Aaah!" the serpent sighed.

Serpent: "Mmm! Mmm! Mmm! Will you take a look at that delicious looking, mouth-watering fruit over yonder."

Narrator: Naturally, the woman, Eve's attention was roused to curiosity.

Eve: "You talkin' to me?"

Serpent: "Why not, ya' standin' here."

Eve: "Well, you could look, but don't touch! 'Cause God said, "hands off.""

Eve: "You touch; you die!"

Narrator: The serpent chuckled.

Serpent: "Is that right! Woman, you know you want it! Besides, if you don't tell, I won't be tellin'."

Serpent: "Anyway, God knows that if you try it, your senses will be enhanced and you will be as a goddess."

Narrator: The woman giggled.

Eve: "Me, a goddess? Now that's tight."

Narrator: The serpent responded with a bit of sarcasm.

Serpent: "Yea, imagine that! Besides, you know God was just jokin'. I mean, who ever heard of such a thing?"

Eve: "Yea, I hear ya'. But the thing is, I don't think he was laughin' when he said it."

Serpent: "Listen up! I know somethin' 'bout God that you're yet to find out."

Eve: "Yea, what's that?"

Serpent: "He's a pushover! Looka here, God loves you so much that he wouldn't dream of kickin' you and boy genius to the curb, and that's the god honest truth."

Eve: "Ya know! you've got a point."

Eve: "Wait up! Lemme get my 'boo,' he might want somma' this."

Serpent: "O' goody, a threesome; now we can have a party."

Narrator: "Immediately after the lure of temptation sin was conceived, and the results gave birth to death.

Conclusion: Resist the devil, again...and again...and again, and he will flee from you (Jas. 4:7).

The End!

Point of Contact

A person with no direction is like a person in a boxing match without boxing gloves. No course of action means TKO. Well, without the Sword of the Spirit, the Word of God, there goes another technical knock out.

———

Guilt

Into Thine hand I commit My Spirit: Thou hast redeemed me, O Lord God of truth (Ps. 31:5).

He shall redeem their soul from deceit and violence: and precious shall their blood be in His sight (Ps. 72:14).

Bless the Lord, O my soul: Who redeemeth my life from destruction: who crowneth thee with loving kindness and tender mercies (Ps. 103:1-4).

In all their affliction, He was afflicted, and the angel of His presence saved them: in His love and in His pity, He redeemed them; and He bare them, and carried them all the days of old (Is. 63:9).

Christ hath redeemed us from the curse of the law, being made a curse for us (Gal. 3:13).

Stand fast therefore in the liberty wherewith Christ has made us free, and be not entangled again with the yoke of bondage (Gal. 5:1).

Hakuna Matata

For the law of the Spirit of life in Christ Jesus hath made me free from the law of sin and death (Rom. 8:2).

No cares, no worries, no battles for the rest of your days... well, not exactly. However, you'll be at peace knowing there is no condemnation to us who are in Christ Jesus (Rom. 8:1).

In the movie *Lion King*, whenever the cub Simba realized that everything around him was falling apart he ran away, hoping to escape the memory of a very painful moment in time. When I lost my mother, I was devastated. It did appear that everything we shared together – the good times, and bad, the inspiring lectures, even our leisurely walks – were gone forever. You see, like the young lion in the movie, I too felt responsible for the accident that caused her death.

One evening, after phoning her from my job, she showed up minutes earlier than usual and after the two of us drove away, an eighteen-wheeler, that perhaps would have missed her, slammed into us on the driver's side. Whenever she noticed him coming at us, she gasped, "Oh my God" This was as if to say, "I can't believe I'm going to be hit." I remember turning my head to look at this large shiny silver vehicle, assuming that the driver would slam down on the breaks, causing the wheeler to stop just in time, but he didn't. He later said that he was unable to stop.

Immediately after the incident, I was carried away to safety in an ambulance while my mother's body remained there lifeless. Unlike the young cub in the movie, I tried to tell myself that this was a normal occurrence; after all, bad things happen. So for years I held on to this mindset, hoping that perhaps this way of thinking might keep me from tipping the scales and losing it altogether. But, time led to another way of thinking and there I was at the brink of despair.

Being unable to take it anymore, I fell to my knees sobbing hysterically when, at that moment, the Comforter came by. I knew that He was near because I felt a peace and assurance unlike anything that any Psychologist could provide. I thank God that He doesn't judge matters based on the thoughts or theories of men. For, He heard my cry from within; He ministered to me and healed me. Immediately after, He pronounced me not guilty. It's been years since that time, and I thank God for a peace, not of this world.

Yes, there is a place not far away, where we can find peace from life's storms, and strength for whatever comes our way. There is a place in God that shelters you from the affects of distressing circumstances; it is known as God's secret place. When you find it, no one has to tell you so, and no one can take it away. In that secret place, you'll discover the true meaning of the words Hakuna Matata.

Point of Contact

Now, all you have to concern yourself with is forgiving yourself.

Chapter Twenty-Four

Holiness

I *speak after the manner of men because of the infirmity of your flesh: for as ye have yielded your members servants to uncleanness and to iniquity unto iniquity, even so now yield your members servants to righteousness unto holiness (Rom. 6:19).*

I beseech you therefore, brethren, by the mercies of God, that ye present your bodies a living sacrifice, holy acceptable unto God, which is your reasonable service (Rom. 12:1).

And be not conformed to this world: but be ye transformed by the renewing of your mind, that ye may prove what is that good, and acceptable, and perfect will of God (Rom. 12:2).

Because it is written, Be ye holy; for I am holy (1 Pet. 1:15-16).

It's Gettin' Hot In Here

That I may know Him, and the power of His resurrection, and the fellowship of His suffering, being made conformable unto His death (Phil. 3:10).

What is holiness, and how does one maintain this consecrated lifestyle? Holiness is something your mom could never really define, something you could not get a feel for by reading religious books, or starring at stained glass windows. It isn't something you can purchase from a store, or talk yourself into. It's more than putting on a show by pretending to be devout, or isolating yourself from the world around you.

When I was growing up, the holy walk was vital, and well, if you really want to know, somewhat enforced; at least from my little corner of the world. In Catholicville, I assumed God was pleased with an unpainted face, a nice glance instead of a stare, and pastels instead of the "I'm coming out" bold colors. This way of life, with its dos and don'ts gave a whole new meaning to the words "cleanliness is next to Godliness."

Therefore, I assumed this pathway would certainly pave my way to heaven. But, this was not so, because later I learned that my idea of holiness was meaningless in the eyes of God. The overbearing weight of forever watching your p's and q's, never wanting to step out of makeup, for fear of those holier than thou fingers pointing in your direction with a smile and a curse. That does nothing but further baffle the mind. You become so frustrated with the thought of keeping up, until you finally submit yourself to letting your hair down, stripping off the clothes, and doing whatever comes natural. Uh-oh, it's getting' hot in here; now, what did I do with my clothes?

Into Character

Years later, whenever my relationship with Christ developed into something more than a simple "Hail Mary," the Spirit of God ushered me into a consummated rapport with the Lord, and through it a yearning to go after the things of God, without the weight of obligation. It may have become a personal decision and a joy to surrender self – body, mind, and spirit – to the Lord, that He might transform me into a vessel of holiness.

Point of Contact

Holiness is a lifestyle! It is not necessarily about religion or anything else that we may have learned from the old school. Be excited over the fact that God chose you to walk after Him.

Women

Who can find a virtuous woman? For her price is far above rubies. The heart of her husband doth safely trust in her, so that he shall have no need of spoil. She will do him good and not evil all the days of her life (Prov. 31:10-12).

Many daughters have done virtuously, but thou excellest them all (Prov. 31:29).

Favour is deceitful, and beauty is vain: but a woman that feareth the Lord, she shall be praised (Prov. 31:30).

For the Lord hath called thee as a woman forsaken and grieved in spirit, and a wife of youth, when thou wast refused, saith thy God (Is. 54:6).

So God created man in His own image, in the image of God created He him; male and female created He them (Gen. 1:27).

"Sing and rejoice, O daughter of Zion: for, lo, I come, and I will dwell in the midst of thee," saith the Lord (Zec. 2:10).

Daughters

...These daughters are My daughters (Gen. 31:43).

I believe, women, like men, are called of God to fulfill a great commission on the earth. However, like (mother) Eve, a great many of us have fallen sway to the enemy's power of suggestion by acting without thinking.

One day, after a period of searching repeatedly for a missing document, I decided to ask the Lord for His help in finding it. No, this was not something out of the ordinary for me, because years ago, I was instructed to do just that whenever a problem about finding a lost item retorted to something like intense frustration.

So rather than searching through a series of words that are usually not found in the dictionary (if you know what I mean), I'd get on my knees and ask the gracious, all-knowing God to help me locate it. Well anyway, during this time it seemed as though I had searched every nook and cranny of my house to find this particular document, but all to no avail. After a little while, I heard His still calm voice say to me: "You'll find it where you least expect."

I thought for a moment, then out of frustration answered in ignorance saying, "Really, Lord! I do not expect to find it any place... not here anyway." Again His still, calm voice spoke saying, "Then you cannot expect to find it."

One Sunday morning, after church service, I met up with an old acquaintance and while walking to my car, we greeted each other excitedly, then began a conversation about the many things that had taken place in our lives since we last saw one another. She was quite anxious to tell me about the goings-on in her life, making sure I understood all the details. However, after a little while, her facial expression changed; actually, she looked disturbed as she confessed her many insecurities and weaknesses.

In my attempt to share words of wisdom and encouragement from my own experiences, her voice grew the louder. It had appeared to me that although she wanted a way out of her dilemma, she did not expect to find one.

Like the document that I had misplaced, the answer to her problem was practically in the palm of her hands. But, she was blind to it.

You know, whenever I stood still long enough and allowed the Spirit of God to help me be focused, He directed my attention to that document which was actually right there in the next room lying on a shelf; I gasped when I saw it.

You know, some times, the most obvious place to find God's peace is buried under many anxieties and cares of this life. Guilt is one of the keys that the enemy uses to lock the door and keep us from reaching abundant living; therefore, we seldom find the peace of God.

Point of Contact

God thought so much of the female gender that He took His time forming us. Don't let the creativity of the Almighty God go to waste in you. Each day, we should remind ourselves that we are anointed, and here to do great exploits.

Men

For Thou hast made him a little lower than the angels, and hast crowned him with glory and honour. Thou madest him to have dominion over the works of Thy hands; Thou hast put all things under His feet (Ps. 8:5-6).

A man's pride shall bring him low: but honour shall uphold the humble in spirit (Prov. 29:23).

Who is as the wise man? And who knoweth the interpretation of a thing? A man's wisdom maketh his face to shine, and the boldness of his face shall be changed (Eccl. 8:1).

How can one enter into a strongman's house, and spoil his goods, except he first bind the strongman? And then he will spoil his house (Mt. 12:29).

For as by one man's disobedience many were made sinners, so by the obedience of One shall many be made righteous (Rom. 5:19).

Salt of the Earth

Ye are the salt of the earth: but if the salt has lost its savour, wherewith shall it be salted? (Mt. 5:13).

"Are you a man or a mouse?" Remember this phrase? It's describes those who could not take authority over their surroundings, perhaps due to the fear of a person or particular task that appeared overwhelming. But, God created man in His image to be like Himself: God made man master over all the earth (Gen. 1:26).

Since the beginning of time, God had ordained man to be the salt of the earth, and since the beginning of time man grew timid in his search to lead, through Godly authority. Take Adam, who being fully aware of God's death penalty, stood there speechless while his wife Eve fell under the devil's coaxing; that which nearly landed all of creation in a lake of fire. He further displayed no authority over his right to guide the affairs of his house. Surely with the authority that was given to Adam by God, he could have stood up against the devil's attack, rebuked him and sent him into the lake of fire right then.

Therefore, he would have rescued his wife Eve from the responsibility of a job that did not belong to her as woman. While we're on the subject, what about king Ahab, in the book of 1 Kings, whose wife, Jezebel managed to take control of most of his affairs, as though God had asked her to rule the world. However, if it were not for Ahab's own wickedness in idol worship, perhaps he would have been able to take his stand as a man, and manage his business in the fullness of his calling.

Nonetheless, God made man to be the head – a priest before the Lord – that he might effectively guide the comings and goings of his area of dominion.

Point of Contact

Seek after the things of God as you would seek after buried treasure. Then go after understanding; it's powerful!

INDEX

Other Books Available
from Lighthouse Publications

These and other Christian books from Lighthouse Publications are available at participating local Christian bookstores, Amazon.com & Bn.com.

To order books directly from Lighthouse Publications:
Visit www.Lighthouse-Publications.com

Lighthouse Publications
2028 Larkin Avenue
Elgin, IL 60123
(847) 697-6788

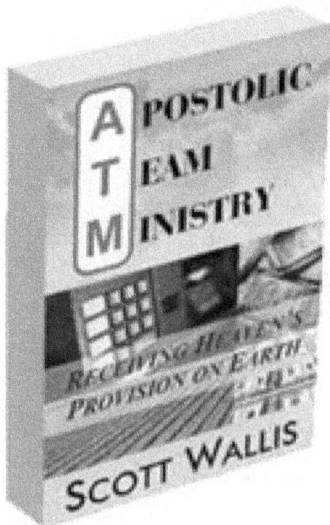

Apostolic Team Ministry

Pastor/Prophet Scott Wallis provides practical answers to the questions that many believers have, such as: "How can I overcome lack in my life?" Learn why apostles are so important to the purpose and plans of God, and how apostolic teams release tremendous supernatural power and wealth into the Church.

Author: Scott Wallis
Retail Price: $11.99
ISBN: 0964221128

The Third Reformation is Coming

Prophetic leaders have been declaring for several years that a third reformational movement of the Holy Spirit was about to begin. Find out what this third reformation is and how it will radically change the Church and your life.

Author: Scott Wallis
Retail Price: $9.99
ISBN: 0964221144

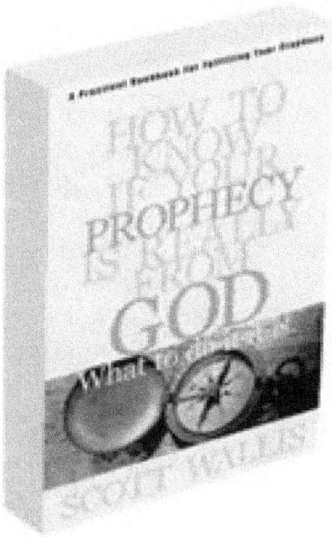

How to Know if Your Prophecy is Really from God

One of the most important books on prophecy available for Believers. If you have ever received a prophetic word, then this book will help you discern if that word was from God, and if it was, what to do with it to see if fulfilled.

Author: Scott Wallis
Retail Price: $11.99
ISBN: 1931232415

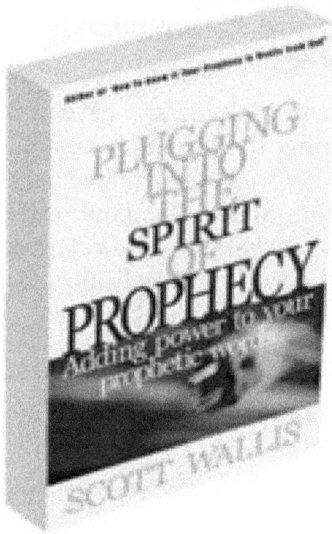

Plugging into the Spirit of Prophecy

God has designed every believer to walk in the prophetic. You can learn how to flow in the Holy Spirit of prophecy. This exciting book will teach you how to do this and more. You will experience God's awesome power through the prophetic word.

Author: Scott Wallis
Retail Price: $11.99
ISBN: 1931232210

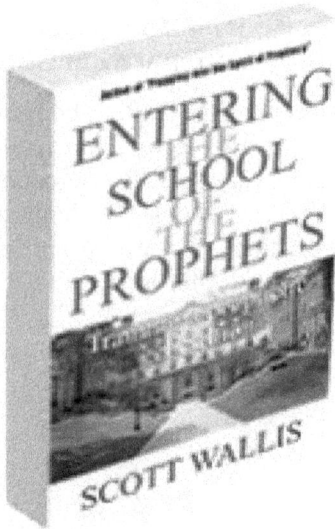

Entering the School of the Prophets

Scott Wallis's third book in his series on understanding prophetic ministry that answers questions regarding the prophetic office and its value to the Body of Christ today. A great resource for those desiring to understand more about the prophetic office and ministry.

Author: Scott Wallis
Retail Price: $12.99
ISBN: 1-933656-04-2

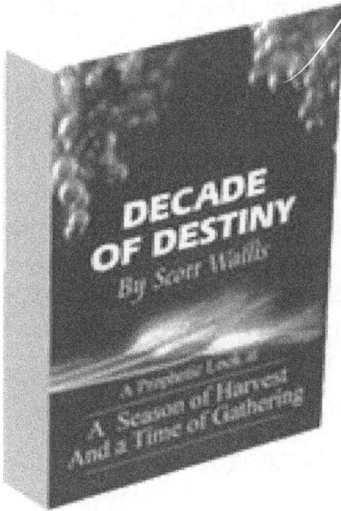

Decade of Destiny

A powerful prophetic word detailing what God is doing in our days. First written in 1991, this timeless book has proven to be an accurate window into the future. Discover what God is saying to His Church today!

Author: Scott Wallis
Retail Price: $11.99
ISBN: 0964221195

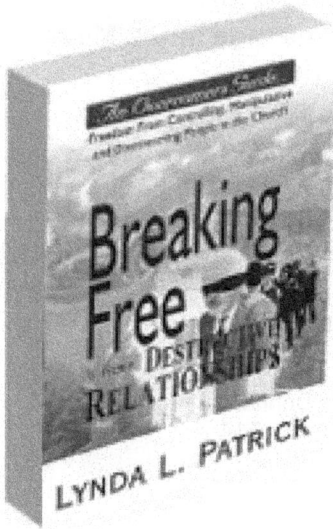

Breaking Free from Destructive Relationships

Lynda Patrick explains the facets of spiritual control and abuse that so many believers face, giving insights into the beginnings and outcomes. She exposes the Jezebel spirit, and articulates the remedies that will "set free the mind and spirit...to the eternal purposes that were predetermined...before the abuse even took place."

Authors: Lynda L. Patrick
Retail Price: $14.99
ISBN: 193365600X

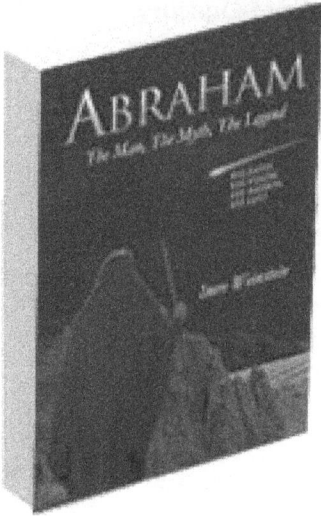

Abraham: The Man, The Myth, The Legend

A fictional account of Abraham's early years, based in a Biblical worldview. All the wonder of God's redemption in the life of a young pagan man, his glorious romance with Sarai, the exciting action of battles and rescue encounters, and his discovery of the one true God of the universe.

Author: Imre Weinstein
Retail Price: $19.99
ISBN: 1933656018

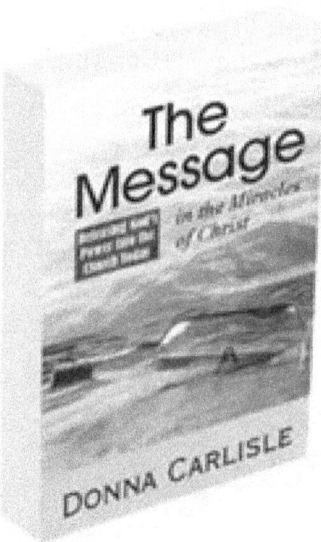

The Message in the Miracles of Christ

Recently, researchers have discovered that there may be hidden coded messages in the actual text of the Bible. Could it be that the miracles of Jesus also reveal hidden messages of what God is doing in our day? Discover the answer as you read this exciting book!

Author: Donna Carlisle
Retail Price: $14.99
ISBN: 0964221136

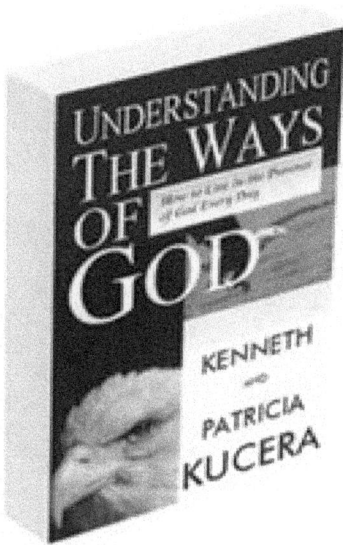

Understanding the Ways of God

You can understand the mysteries behind God's ways. No longer wonder why God does what He does – you can know. As you read this exciting book, you will learn secret after secret of walking in the ways of God. Unlock the potential God has placed inside of you as you learn the ways of God!

Authors: Kenneth & Patricia Kucera
Retail Price: $11.99
ISBN: 0964221152

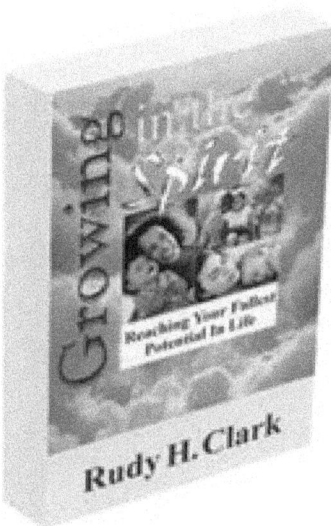

Growing in the Spirit

Taking from life examples, Pastor/Prophet Rudy Clark reveals principles of spiritual growth. Through many life lessons, God has taught Reverend Clark the values and virtues that have made him the man he is today. Experience freedom as you learn how to reach your fullest potential.

Author: Rudy H. Clark
Retail Price: $14.99
ISBN: 0964221160

www.ingramcontent.com/pod-product-compliance
Lightning Source LLC
LaVergne TN
LVHW091249080426
835510LV00007B/185